FORGIVENESS

An Act of Grace and Mercy

Bobbie Sorrill Patterson

Woman's Missionary Union
Birmingham, Alabama

Woman's Missionary Union
P. O. Box 830010
Birmingham, AL 35283-0010

©2001 by Woman's Missionary Union
All rights reserved. First printing 2001
Printed in the United States of America
Woman's Missionary Union® and WMU® are registered trademarks.

All rights reserved. No part of this publication may be reproduced, stored in a retrieval system, or transmitted in any form or by any means—electronic, mechanical, photocopying, recording, or otherwise—without the prior written permission of the publisher.

Dewey Decimal Classification: 234.5
Subject Headings: FORGIVENESS
   REPENTANCE AND RECONCILIATION
   (THEOLOGY)

Unless otherwise noted, Scripture quotations are from *Contemporary English Version*. Copyright ©American Bible Society 1991. Used by permission.
   Scripture quotations identified NIV are from the Holy Bible, New International Version. Copyright © 1973, 1978, 1984 International Bible Society. Used by permission of Zondervan Bible Publishers.
   Scripture quotations from *The Message*. Copyright ©1993, 1994, 1995. Used by permission of NavPress Publishing Group.

Design by Janell Young

ISBN: 1-56309-487-8
W014107•0701•5M1

In memory of Art Patterson,
my mentor and companion
in Bible study

Contents

Preface ix

Introduction xiii

1: Why Do We Need Forgiveness? 1

2: What Are Sin's Consequences? 12

3: How Did God Forgive Sin in the Old Testament? . .24

4: Whom Did God Forgive in the Old Testament? . . .46

5: What Difference Did Jesus' Life Make

in Forgiveness? 61

6: What Did Jesus Teach About Forgiveness? 73

7: How Did Jesus Model Forgiveness? 86

8: Whom Did God Forgive in the New Testament? . .100

9: What Is Involved When We Forgive Others? 114

10: Why Is It Important to Forgive Ourselves? 126

11: What Does Prayer Have to Do with

Forgiveness? 137

12: How Can I Live a Forgiven Life? 150

Preface

When the publisher asked me to write one of the books in the "Timeless Bible Truths for the Twenty-First-Century Woman" series, I was excited. The subject of forgiveness immediately challenged me; but I was delighted to accept the challenge. You see, I've been forgiven and have forgiven others, and the personal joy I felt as I was forgiven caused me to want that same opportunity for others.

Questions flooded my mind and heart. What does forgiveness mean? What are basic concepts one needs to explore about forgiveness? What does the Bible have to say about this subject? What does forgiveness really mean to the twenty-first-century Christ follower?

When I am searching for a definition of anything, I always consult the dictionary first. Dictionary definitions say to forgive is "to give up resentment of or claim to requital for"; "to grant relief from payment of"; "to cease to feel resentment against." The adjective *forgiving* means "willing or able to forgive"; "allowing room for error or weakness."[1]

Frankly, these definitions were not especially helpful to me in understanding the Christian concept of forgiveness. Forgiveness has both divine and human dimensions and the dictionary definitions were more human than divine.

From the divine perspective, forgiveness is an act or gift of God. God in His grace and mercy blots out forever the sins of His people when they confess and repent and accept the salvation He offers through Jesus Christ. He no longer holds us accountable. He restores fellowship with us and reestablishes a relationship with us. Because of God's supreme sacrifice of His Son, Jesus Christ, God transfers each of us from spiritual death to spiritual life. As a result, we can live daily the forgiven life of freedom and dignity, released from guilt, and set free for service.

Christian forgiveness also has a human dimension. Human forgiveness is an act of grace and attitude of mercy toward others who have wronged us, which restores the relationship and fellowship. Through forgiveness, we no longer hold wrongful acts against others. We pardon or excuse wrongs, cancel debts, give up any claim for revenge or resentment, and forge a new start in attitudes and actions.

This Bible study explores 12 concepts related to forgiveness:

- Why we need forgiveness
- Consequences of sin
- God's provision of a sacrificial system
- God's forgiveness demonstrated with David
- God's perfect and final sacrifice
- Jesus' teachings about forgiveness
- Jesus as a model of forgiveness
- God's forgiveness demonstrated with Peter and Paul
- Forgiving others
- Forgiving self
- The relationship of prayer to forgiveness
- Living out the forgiven life

Though a thorough study of forgiveness is extremely difficult, I have come to three fairly simple conclusions. First, forgiveness is indeed a timeless truth for the twenty-first-century Christ follower. It is a bedrock principle of one's Christian faith, so needed in today's complex world. Second, for me forgiveness is personal, not a philosophical concept. God has forgiven me. And with God's grace and mercy, I can forgive others and myself.

Third, forgiveness is experiential, something I can feel, touch, and experience. Though the awesome, heavenly God is in control of and loves the entire world, I personally have experienced God's grace, mercy, and forgiveness. And, I must personally forgive those who have wronged me—others or myself, even as God has forgiven me.

The Apostle Paul summed up the essence of forgiveness, being acceptable to God, and the new life in Christ in his letter to the Romans.

"But God showed how much he loved us by having Christ die for us, even though we are sinful. But there is more! Now that God has accepted us because Christ sacrificed his life's blood, we will also be kept safe from God's anger. Even when we were God's enemies, he made peace with us, because his Son died for us. Yet something even greater than friendship is ours. Now that we are at peace with God, we will be saved by his Son's life. And in addition to everything else, we are happy because God sent our Lord Jesus Christ to make peace with us" (Rom. 5:8–11).

My prayer as you read this book is that you will experience the forgiveness our God so graciously and mercifully gives, extend forgiveness to others and to yourself, and victoriously live a forgiven life.

BOBBIE SORRILL PATTERSON

[1] *Merriam-Webster's Collegiate Dictionary,* 10th ed., s.v. "forgive"; "forgiving."

Introduction

Forgiveness is an act of grace and mercy on God's part. Forgiveness pardons wrongs, reestablishes broken relationships, and includes a new start in attitudes and actions. God's grace took the initiative to provide us with undeserved forgiveness.

The Old Testament shows us Israel's experience of what God is like and what they, as worshipers of God, should be like. God chose Israel as a special people and had a unique relationship with them. He promised to bless these people, to make of them a great nation, and to bless other nations through them. These blessings are described in agreements or covenants, beginning with Abraham and continuing through the Old Testament. Though God's chosen people struggled to keep their part of the covenant and often disobeyed, God was ever faithful to forgive, guide, and instruct. He provided us with covenant grace in the Old Testament.

In the New Testament, God continued to act with grace in providing forgiveness even when people broke the covenant. God demonstrates His forgiving grace and mercy supremely in the Christ Event of the New Testament. In a sense, God made a new agreement with His people. And, He completed putting His plan of forgiveness and salvation into effect with His incarnation and the death and resurrection of Jesus Christ, our Savior and Lord.

Forgiveness is a beautiful concept. But it is more than a concept. It is an act of our heavenly Father that is life-changing and transformational. In his book *Reaching for the Invisible God*, Christian writer Philip Yancey describes grace as water that flows to the lowest part. Indeed, grace is like water for me personally as it trickles and rushes simultaneously to my innermost being, cleansing and forgiving. And, it flows to the depths of depravity, sin, and wickedness in our lost and hurting world. God's forgiving grace is clothed in compassion, love, sympathy, and deep caring summarized in the word *mercy*. That's what this book is about.

This book is divided into three parts: Chapters 1–3 offer basic, foundational truths from Scripture related to God's forgiveness. Chapters 4–8 offer biblical models, examples, case studies, and applications. And chapters 9–12 deal with the human implications of forgiveness and call us to forgiving attitudes, actions, and practices.

Each chapter poses a question and answers that question in summary form, leading into the more involved explanations and ideas which follow. Yet no chapter is complete until you, the reader, answers the questions at the end of that chapter and applies those answers to your life.

1

Why Do We Need Forgiveness?

Because we have sinned against God and others.

As a 9-year-old girl, brought up in the church, I was increasingly overcome by feelings of guilt and wrongdoing. In my mind and heart I was a bad girl who did bad things. I had a strong sense of needing God to do something to me, to change me somehow. I was really dealing with a concept, sin, which I did not completely understand at the time. However, in a simple way I began to understand that sin is the reason we need forgiveness. And since sin caused the need for forgiveness, it became essential for me as I matured to understand the nature of sin, the consequences of sin, and God's provision for dealing with sin.

Sin lies at the core of all of our problems. Because we are humans and by nature sinful, we rebel

Genesis 1:24–31; 2:7,18–25; 3:1–6; 3:7–24; 4–9

Exodus 19; 24; 32; 23:7; 1:18

Leviticus 11:45

Deuteronomy 6:24–25

Joshua 24

Psalms 32; 51:1–7; 103:1–12; 5:5; 7:11

Isaiah 1:18–20

Nahum 1:3

Matthew 5:21–22,27–28; 15:18–20; 28:18–20

John 8:34

Romans 7:23–25; 3:23; 12:1–2; 5:10; 8:7; 5:12; 6:6; 6:23; 7:17; 7:20; 3:9–23

Galatians 6:7

Hebrews 12:1

James 2:9–11; 14–15; 4:17

1 John 5:17

against God, willfully disobey Him, and choose to satisfy our own desires and wills rather than God's. Sin breaks our relationship and fellowship with God and creates within us a sense of personal guilt and blame of others. Sin also breaks relationship and fellowship with other people.

Without sin and the devastation it causes, we would have no need for forgiveness. But, our God is a God of holiness, love, mercy, and grace. He wants to restore a relationship and fellowship with His children. I know now that as a child, I was reaching out to God but He also was reaching out to me. Sin had become real to me. God made His forgiveness real too.

The Reality of Sin

Sin is real in each person's life and defying the devil and sin becomes a daily challenge. It is by no means an easy challenge, but a life-threatening issue. Basically sin is rebellion and disobedience against God. Even the dictionary relates sin to an act against God, saying sin is "an offense against religious or moral law," a "transgression of the law of God," and "a vitiated [weak, faulty] state of human nature in which the self is estranged from God."[1]

Sin is a difficult concept to understand, as is the concept of forgiveness. The Bible gives no formal definition of sin. However, God's written Word is in essence the story of the sin of people and the forgiveness of God. Sin capitalizes on human weakness and centers in acts or attitudes of rebellion by people against God and others. God gives people freedom of choice. Sin causes individuals by choice to miss the mark of God's will and purpose for their lives and instead surrender to the power of evil. And, though we don't understand the concept of sin, we continue to sin.

It helps my understanding of sin to think about it on a personal level in my own life or within my environment rather than philosophically or theologically. What does sin mean to you and me? Sometimes, especially as young Christians but also as more mature Christ followers, we are prone to view sin as the more horrible transgressions or so-called gross sins such as murder, suicide, adultery, rape, incest, wild and wasteful lifestyles, dissipated living, immorality, infidelity in marriage, racism, drunkenness, or deliberate abuse of one's body. These sins I can see readily in others or in society but I am not always so quick to see them in my own life. Some sins seem more serious than others do because their consequences are more serious.

There are no degrees in sin, however. God does not classify sins as large or small, heavy or light. Sin is a child's willful disobedience of parents, but it is also an adult who breaks a law, or someone who defies God's will. Sin is thinking evil thoughts about others, accumulating more and more material possessions for one's own purposes and not for God's use, gluttony, bad attitudes, selfishness, being self-centered, participating in or even watching activities that are harmful to one's body and soul, jealousy, and on and on. We may think of these as more subtle sins, which are sometimes even more tempting to those of us who consider ourselves good and righteous.

There are also serious sins of omission. Sometimes I find myself failing to follow God's will for my life or my day. I refuse to take advantage of opportunities He gives me to minister and to witness. Sometimes I say no to doing good rather than yes. Any transgression of God's will is sin—big and serious sins, subtle sins, sins of omission. James 2:9–11 says:

"But if you treat some people better than others, you have done wrong, and the Scriptures teach that you have

sinned. If you obey every law except one, you are still guilty of breaking them all. The same God who told us to be faithful in marriage also told us not to murder. So even if you are faithful in marriage, but murder someone, you still have broken God's Law."

What is sin? It is an action or attitude that disobeys God or fails to do what is good or right. It is rebellion against God's will. At the heart of sin is selfishness, centering our lives in self rather than in God. Our own evil desires tempt us, drag us away, and entice us (James 1:14–15; Rom. 7:23–25). No one else or nothing else is responsible. We fail to do what we know is right (James 4:17). Sin always brings consequences and we suffer those consequences (Rom. 3:23), a concept we will deal with in the next chapter.[2]

The tragedy is that all sin separates people from God. But God can and will forgive all sin.

The First Act of Disobedience

How did sin come about in the first place? Genesis 3 describes the setting: On the sixth day of creation after making day and night, the sky, land and water, plants and animals, God created a man and a woman in His own image and gave them the freedom of choice and a rational, emotional, and moral nature. God directed the man and woman to fill the earth with other people and rule over all the other creatures. God was pleased with what He had done. Thus, these humans enjoyed the supreme position in all of creation (Gen. 1:24–31; 2:7, 18–25).

God placed the man and woman in a garden called Eden, which was full of beautiful trees. In Hebrew, the word for *Eden* means pleasure or delight.[3] Two trees stood in the middle of the garden. One of these trees gave life, the other the power to know the difference between right and wrong. God said the man and woman would die if they ate fruit from the tree of knowledge of good and evil. God placed these two, whom we know as Adam and Eve, in the garden to take care of it and to look after it.

Think about the indescribable and idyllic life Adam and Eve enjoyed. They were made in God's image, that is, "like" Him. They had a beautiful place to live and a special relationship with God, and they represented God on earth by ruling over the other creatures.

Their perfect life was marred and destroyed when Adam and Eve disobeyed God's command. God told them to enjoy everything in the garden, but not to eat fruit from the tree of knowledge of good and evil that would let them know the difference between right and wrong.

You know the story well. The serpent, sneakier than any other wild animal, evil, and usually considered to be Satan, enticed Eve to eat of the forbidden fruit. Satan often seems to disguise himself. The fruit was beautiful and tasty. Eve wanted to know what God knew. She ate of the fruit, but also enticed Adam to eat some too.

God had given the crown of His creation a choice and they chose to disobey. This willful decision was sin. At that point an act of disobedience set aside God's original purpose for people and sin infected humanity forever (Gen. 3:1–6).

Adam and Eve suffered the consequences of sin. First, they realized they were naked, felt guilty, and hid from God. Second, their perfect relationship with God was broken. God banished Adam and Eve from the Garden of Eden forever. They blamed others for their sin. Adam blamed Eve and Eve blamed the serpent. They were separated from God and lost fellowship with Him. When they chose Satan's will rather than God's will, they died spiritually. The image was tarnished. And after that, Adam and Eve lived a life of hardship, the woman with pain in childbirth forever and the man with toil to grow food forever. They lived under the wrath of God and would ultimately die and turn back into the soil from which God had made them (Gen. 3:7–24).

Sin multiplied and spread rapidly. The descendants of Adam and Eve continued to sin because it had become their nature. Their son Cain murdered his brother Abel. The people on earth were evil. Cruelty and violence were widespread and God was sorry He had made humans. God destroyed all humanity with a flood, sparing only Noah and his family (Gen. 4–9). From this point on in human history, sin infected human beings for all time.

Does the story of Adam and Eve apply to us today? Does it have meaning for us? Does it help in our understanding of sin? We, too, are created in God's image and can make choices, think, reason, and feel. We inherited the desire to sin and be enticed by it from all of our ancestors, starting with Adam and Eve way back at the beginning of human existence on earth. We, too, disobey God, feel guilty, and try to hide from Him. And, tragically, we, too, let sin separate us from God and break our fellowship with Him. We let it tamper with the most precious things we have in life.

A Biblical View of Sin

The Old Testament shows the progression of people's understanding of sin. The Jewish mind in biblical times, unlike most today, could deal with seemingly mutually exclusive ideas. Therefore, they could understand that people inherited a sinful nature from Adam and Eve, but still had freedom of choice, hence a choice about sin.

God's standard of righteousness in the Old Testament was the law. Any violation of God's righteous nature or of the law was considered sin (Deut. 6:24–25). Any deviation from God's criterion of holiness (Lev. 11:45) was sin. God also established a covenant with Israel (Ex. 19; 24; Josh. 24). Each year on the Day of Atonement, the people went through a covenant renewal. Any breach of the covenant was sin.[4]

Many Old Testament examples reveal that no sin is too great for God to forgive. He forgave the Israelites, wandering in the wilderness for 40 years, when they made an idol shaped like a golden calf, sacrificed offerings to the idol, and engaged in a drunken orgy. At the time, Moses was on Mount Sinai getting the Ten Commandments (Ex. 32). God forgave His chosen people over and over again as they disobeyed Him while they traveled through the wilderness and prepared to enter the Promised Land.

God forgave the Israelites during the dark ages of the judges, during the leadership vacuum after Joshua and before the kings. He forgave the evil, sin, and debauchery committed during the days of the kings of Israel and Judah. He spoke words of condemnation through His prophets. Isaiah was explicit about Judah's guilt and the terrible condition into which the nation had fallen. However, God extended this invitation to Judah:

"'Come now, let us reason together,' says the Lord. 'Though your sins are like scarlet, they shall be as white as snow; though they are red as crimson, they shall be like wool. If you are willing and obedient, you will eat the best from the land; but if you resist and rebel, you will be devoured by the sword' For the mouth of the Lord has spoken" (Isa. 1:18–20 NIV).

Chapter 4 explores God's demonstration of forgiveness with the king David. David wrote many of the psalms and these psalms testify to God's forgiveness of David's terrible sins (Psalm 32; 51:1–7; 103:1–12).

An article in *The Learning Bible* describes sin in the Old Testament in seven ways:

1. Breaking the Law of Moses, failing to live as God intended, or turning one's back on God to follow other gods. We, too, are prone to live our lives as we want to rather than following God's will and direction. And, we worship many other gods such as self, power, money, possessions, abilities, even family.
2. Defying or rebelling against God resulting in a broken relationship with Him. Sin today still results in a broken relationship with God.
3. Acts of violence against others or ways of secretly hurting or harming others. Even as Christ followers, we are masters at hurting other persons, both overtly and covertly.
4. Not following the Law of Moses by failing to offer correct sacrifices, thus being unfit to come into God's presence. Though we no longer are bound by the Old Testament sacrifices, we are instructed to daily offer our bodies as living sacrifices (Rom. 12:1–2). Do we?
5. Pride in the wrongs that come out of an evil human heart. Pride is as much a part of our contemporary lives as it was in biblical times.
6. Failure to live up to or reflect God's glory. No sin honors and glorifies God.
7. Consequences of one person's sin on many other persons.[5] If I sin, it affects my family, friends, co-workers, fellow believers, and others in my sphere of influence.

Different Hebrew words give significant insights into the meaning of sin. One word means missing the mark such as when an archer misses the target with his bow and arrow. Other words mean stepping across the line, any action that opposed God's standard of righteousness, evilness or wickedness, a crooked or corrupt spirit, unclean or impure, unbelief or lack of faith, and lust.[6]

In the New Testament, sin has a deeper meaning. Jesus is the standard of righteousness and sin is defined against that standard. He lived a perfect, pure, and sinless life.

Chapter 6 explores what Jesus taught about sin and forgiveness. In the New Testament sin is viewed as lack of fellowship with God. Jesus taught that sin is a condition of the heart and involves inner motives (Matt. 5:21–22, 7–28; 15:18–20). Sin involves the essential being, the inner core of a person. It is the essence of human nature.

Every person sins and stands in need of forgiveness, and Jesus offers just that. New life in Christ includes resurrection from eternal death and separation from God to eternal life. "Jesus paid the penalty for our sins, and God has a new agreement with people, which includes eternal life. . . . Instead of continuing as slaves to sin, God's new people are now slaves to God."[7]

Both Old Testament law and New Testament grace play a part in our understanding of sin. The Law of Moses initially revealed sin as preparation for pointing to Jesus Christ. The Law showed sin in its true character and gave people a sense of sin and guilt. Because of human nature, we cannot keep the Law. Law does leave a sense of sin and guilt. However, grace or unmerited favor comes through God's provision of Jesus Christ as a perfect sacrifice.

The Bible makes it clear that God abhors sin (Rom. 5:10; 8:7; Psalm 5:5; 7:11). God will punish sin and people must suffer the consequences (Gal. 6:7; Ex. 23:7; Nah. 1:3; Rom. 1:18). Our very nature is to sin (John 8:34; Rom. 5:12; 6:6; 6:23; 7:17; 7:20; Heb. 12:1; 1 John 5:17), but God in His mercy provides a plan of salvation and forgiveness.

Sin Is Universal

No person is exempt from sin. Sin is universal. It is in our very nature. No one is good. Romans 3:9–23 says:
"What does all this mean? Does it mean that we Jews are better off than the Gentiles? No, it doesn't! Jews, as well

as Gentiles, are ruled by sin, just as I have said. The Scriptures tell us, 'No one is acceptable to God! Not one of them understands or even searches for God. They have all turned away and are worthless. There isn't one person who does right. Their words are like an open pit, and their tongues are good only for telling lies. Each word is as deadly as the fangs of a snake, and they say nothing but bitter curses. These people quickly became violent. Wherever they go, they leave ruin and destruction. They don't know how to live in peace. They don't even fear God.' We know that everything in the Law was written for those who are under its power. The Law says these things to stop anyone from making excuses and to let God show that the whole world is guilty. God doesn't accept people simply because they obey the Law. No, indeed! All the Law does is to point out our sin."

No one is righteous or on a par with God's original intentions in creation. We, too, have the freedom of choice. However, we are now by nature sinful. In his book *The Life God Blesses*, Gordon MacDonald expresses it well when he says we are captive to sin and its addictive patterns, habits, moods, and feelings. We are captive to ambitions, desires and lusts, pleasure, things, and appetites. We are sinners by nature and captive to evil.[8]

Though sin is universal and no one is exempt from sinning, it is important to remember that there is hope. God's love, grace, mercy, and forgiveness are also universal. The saving grace of Jesus Christ is available to every person in the world. And, those of us who are Christ followers are charged with the responsibility of taking this message of good news to all peoples on the earth (Matt. 28:18–20).

Questions for Thought and Discussion

1. When did you first become aware of sin in your life? What did you do about it?

2. How would you define sin in a way a person today could understand it? What are some examples?

3. How do we suffer the consequences of sin today? What are some examples of consequences?

4. What is your biblical view of sin? How does sin make you feel? What does it make you want to do?

5. Do you feel hopeless and helpless because of sin? Why or why not?

6. What is the relationship between the universality of sin and the Great Commission in Matthew 28:18–20?

---

[1] *Merriam-Webster's Collegiate Dictionary*, 10th ed., s.v. "sin."
[2] Trent C. Butler, ed., *Holman Bible Dictionary* (Nashville: Holman Bible Publishers, 1991), 1281–83; Karen Dockery, Johnnie Godwin, and Phyllis Godwin, *Holman Student Bible Dictionary* (Nashville: Holman Bible Publishers, 1993), 212–13.
[3] *The Learning Bible*, Contemporary English Version (New York: American Bible Society, 2000), 43.
[4] Butler, *Holman Bible Dictionary,* 1281–83.
[5] *The Learning Bible*, 2089.
[6] Butler, *Holman Bible Dictionary,* 1281–83.
[7] *The Learning Bible*, 2089.
[8] Gordon MacDonald, *The Life God Blesses* (Nashville: Thomas Nelson Publishers, 1994), 81.

2
What Are Sin's Consequences?

A disastrous life and spiritual death apart from God.

Beth (not her real name), a vibrant young Christ follower I know, was eager to open up new avenues of ministry in her church. She had agreed to direct the church's missions program for teenaged girls. Though the leadership team had given her so-called freedom to enlist her own youth leaders, Beth had to run the names by the team first. Imagine Beth's astonishment when the leadership team rejected several leader candidates because they were divorced.

On another occasion, Beth was working with a friend who was campus minister of a nursing school located near Beth's church. Beth and her friend were concerned that the nursing students were not involved in any church and wanted to start a missions group that would meet at the school and involve

Genesis 3:7–10; 3:16–19; 3:23–24

2 Samuel 11–12

1 Kings

2 Kings

1 Chronicles

2 Chronicles

Psalm 1:1–6

Jeremiah 17:1–4,9–11

Amos 5:21–24

Luke 15:13; 15:14; 15:15; 15:28

Romans 3:23; 6:6,16–17,20; 6:13; 6:19; 6:23; 2:1 to 3:8; 1:18 to 3:20; 1:18–32; 3:9

Hebrews 2:14–15

James 4:1–3

Revelation 20:14–15

the students as they could. Beth was certain her church's women's missions group would serve as the sponsor for the student group. When she proposed the idea to the women's group, they rejected the idea soundly. The women feared that sponsorship would lead to opening their homes and the church to the nursing students. This idea was not acceptable because some of the nursing students were black.

Beth had run head on into spiritual blindness in the form of prejudice and racism.

Sin always brings consequences, for believers as well as nonbelievers, and spiritual blindness is but one of those consequences. Because sin is rebellion against God, it is the absolute worst problem for people. It violates and ravishes everything that is holy and righteous, and God is the ultimate holy and righteous being.

Adam and Eve, the first human beings, broke the perfect relationship they had with God in the Garden of Eden. Their choice was to rebel against God's instructions. What consequences did they reap because of their sin? They felt the pain of guilt and shame for the first time (Gen. 3:7–10). They marred their perfect relationship with God. Because of their sin, they would suffer a life of hardship, anxiety, and eventual death (Gen. 3:16–19). They were banished from the ideal Garden of Eden (Gen. 3:23–24).

David, perhaps Israel's greatest king, who united the tribes, received the promise of a royal Messiah in his line. He was a great, godly, and respected leader, but sin brought dire consequences to his life, as 2 Samuel 11–12 reveals.

While his soldiers were off in battle, David sinned by committing adultery with Bathsheba. She was married to Uriah, one of David's soldiers. When Bathsheba became pregnant with David's child, he engineered a plot to send Uriah into battle where he would be killed, an attempt to cover up what he had done. But as David learned, we cannot hide sin from God. God sent the prophet Nathan to confront David and to tell him the consequences he would face because of his sins. The child of this illicit love affair died, and violence, intrigue, sexual sins, and murder ultimately tore David's family apart.

Ten consequences of sin as identified by Billy E. Simmons form the basis for this chapter.[1] Not only are these consequences of sin evident in the lives of Adam, Eve, and David; they are just as real for us today.

Barrier Between God and People

God cannot tolerate that which violates His righteous character, Simmons says, because He is perfect in righteousness. Thus, sin creates a barrier between God and people, all of whom sin. I can think of nothing worse than being separated or out of fellowship with God.

God makes it abundantly clear in His Word that He cannot tolerate sin. Psalm 1 contrasts good and evil persons:

"God blesses those people who refuse evil advice and won't follow sinners or join in sneering at God. Instead, the Law of the Lord makes them happy, and they think about it day and night. They are like trees growing beside a stream, trees that produce fruit in season and always have leaves. Those people succeed in everything they do. That isn't true of those who are evil, because they are like straw blown by the wind. Sinners won't have an excuse on the day of judgment, and they won't have a place with the people of God. The Lord protects everyone who follows him, but the wicked follow a road that leads to ruin" (Psalm 1:1–6). Which kind of person would you rather be?

In Jeremiah 17:1–4,9–11, the prophet repeats God's words of impending punishment on Judah because of their sins. The people of Judah would get what they deserved (v. 10) and discover how foolish they were (v. 11). Their sins had created a barrier between them and God.

Because every person has sinned, all fall short of God's glory as God originally created them (Rom. 3:23). Though created in God's image, no one lives up to or reflects God's glory because of sin. We do not live as God desires, nor do we love Him or others as He commands. Because of sin, people have created a barrier with God.

What do you think of when you hear the word *barrier*? A barrier is something or someone that separates. It may be a wall such as the Berlin Wall, or a huge stone enclosure around a castle. It may be a locked gate or door. It may be a traffic backup or a delayed airline schedule. Or, it may be a receptionist or administrative officer who blocks your ability to see the doctor or CEO. A barrier can be a broken or strained relationship with a significant other. Sin is a barrier that separates us from God, or separates us from another human being.

The Necessity of God's Intervention

Because of sin, God had to intervene in human affairs. People made such a mess of their lives and became so entwined in the entanglements and enticements of sin that they could not get loose from the difficult situation they had created. Human beings cannot "fix" their sin problem. Only the power and love of Almighty God can rectify sin. This was true of Adam and Eve, and it is also true for us.

Sin weighs people down into impossible lives. God Himself has to intervene, and does so with grace and mercy and a wondrous plan of salvation. Even though people receive forgiveness when they accept Jesus Christ as Lord and Savior and continue to be forgiven, they continue to sin. It becomes part of our makeup. We feel helpless when we try so hard to live a better life and follow God's will daily for our lives, yet continue to sin. Only God's intervention can bring about a real change in our lives.

Enslavement to Sin

The consequences of sin reach far both personally and in society. Sin is like an infection. It spreads and gets out of control. If a person or society constantly and consistently follows sin, they become so enmeshed that for all practical purposes, they are enslaved to sin. Sin is like a life-threatening disease that spreads and gets worse.

You know of persons and groups whose sin seems to have enslaved them. The story of the two sons in Luke 15 is one such example, though for one the story has a happy ending. The younger son demanded his inheritance, then wasted all his money in wild living (Luke 15:13). He spent everything he had and was soon starving and in dire straits (v. 14). He suffered one of the greatest indecencies a Jew could experience when he had to take care of pigs (v. 15). While the younger son repented and was happily restored to his father, his brother chose to remain jealous and self-righteous and missed the reunion celebration (v. 28). The story leaves us wondering if the older son ever repented and experienced the joy of restoration with his father and brother.

Contemporary examples also abound. Some women get caught up and trapped in the humiliating, dehumanizing life of prostitution. Alcohol and drug abuse ravish others. One act of theft leads to a lifetime of stealing and deceit. A young person is enticed by riotous living, as was the younger son in Jesus' parable. Or, one gets into a life of total depravity without hope or a way out. Bad habits or negative attitudes and actions may trap others.

Even a society can be enslaved by sin. It happened to the German Nazis before and during World War II with their brutal, inhumane treatment of the Jews. The scars and horror of these acts of inhumanity are still raw today. Ethnic cleansing in Eastern Europe and other parts of the world that has gone on for generations plagues us today with terrible atrocities. Mobs and gangs are into crime and corruption as a seemingly permanent condition. Many politicians and other leaders model immoral lives. Students carry guns into America's schools, shooting and killing fellow students and teachers.

In Romans 6 Paul contrasts a life controlled by sin with a life free in Christ. It is possible, according to Paul, to be a slave to sin (vv. 6,16–17,20) and to be trapped in sin's evil desires (v. 12). It is possible to be an instrument of sin (v. 13), to live an impure and ever-increasing wicked life (v. 19), with death as the wages of sin (v. 23). But, it is also possible to enjoy a forgiven life, one that is free in Jesus Christ.

Spiritual Depravity

A person or society that continues in sin is depraved spiritually, marked by corruption and evil. A spiritually depraved person is bad, crooked, debased, even perverted. This is a terrible description of a person created in the image of God, with freedom of choice, a moral nature, spiritual gifts, and special abilities God could use if sin had not intervened.

According to Simmons, a person or society that continues in sin adds to depravity. This moral crookedness or corruption eventually makes it impossible to reject sin. Sin becomes more than a habit, it becomes a lifestyle.

We need only to read the history of the kings of Israel and Judah in the Old Testament (1 and 2 Kings; 1 and 2 Chron.) to see spiritual depravity illustrated. Some—

actually only a few—of these kings lived for God, but many refused to do so. The wicked kings led the nation astray and into depravity, idolatry, and corruption. God had to deal with the people's sin in powerful ways. During this period of biblical history the prophets spoke forcefully for God about the deplorable spiritual depravity of those times.

And we need only to watch the evening news, peruse the Internet, or read the daily newspaper to realize that depravity, evil, idolatry, and corruption surround us today, both in America and around the world. Sin is as alive and well today as it was in Old Testament times. We can neither deny it nor ignore it.

Spiritual Blindness

Continuing in sin also leads to spiritual blindness. Even as physical blindness handicaps a person, so does spiritual blindness. The corrupting, debilitating influence of sin makes it almost impossible for us to see spiritual truth. A person or society may once have felt a sense of shame and guilt when sinning, but they can reach the point where they are immune and blind to these feelings. None of us is immune to this consequence of sin.

The Old Testament prophet Amos pronounced God's judgment on Israel, the Northern Kingdom, for its complacency, idolatry, and oppression of the poor. These so-called pious, religious people apparently did not really see the plight of the poor. Instead, they had grown complacent and took advantage of the poor. They were cruel, indifferent, and unjust. Amos enumerated the sins of Israel and issued this rousing challenge, as relevant today as it was then:

"I, the Lord, hate and despise your religious celebrations and your times of worship. I won't accept your offerings or animal sacrifices—not even your very best. No more

of your noisy songs! I won't listen when you play your harps. But let justice and fairness flow like a river that never runs dry" (Amos 5:21–24).

Are we blinded to the needs of the poor, homeless, and victims of injustice today? May we, too, be condemned for religious celebrations, times of worship, offerings, and music? Or do we, too, need to let justice and fairness flow like a river that never runs dry? God blesses those who give their lives to help others in need, working with unwed pregnant teenagers, assisting women to rise out of poverty into self-sufficiency, teaching persons to read and write, feeding the hungry, ministering in the prisons, and on and on.

Moral Ineptitude

When a person is inept at something, she or he is incompetent or bungling. Do you or someone you know suffer from poor coordination? What about the incompetence we all sometimes feel when technology races ahead of our skills? Sin's results are similar. As we practice sin more and more, we become inept as far as moral and spiritual values are concerned. If we keep on sinning, sin eventually blurs the distinction between right and wrong, good and evil.

Continuing to sin makes it easier to sin more and to become increasingly inept morally. I remember the time when the Lord's Day was holy. Few stores were open, especially no malls. For many of us, Sunday was truly a day of worship, study, rest, family, and friends. Not so today. Few people today even blink an eye when they stop by a store on the way home from a worship service or spend time doing things that may not honor God. Now it seems as if Sunday is just like any other day. And how easy it is to fall into the trap of watching TV shows and movies that glorify immorality and godless living.

Guilt

Guilt is a huge consequence of sin. Adam and Eve suffered guilt in the Garden of Eden. We need only to read the Psalms to see deep into David's soul and feel the suffering, anguish, and guilt he felt because of his sins. We can relate, because we suffer guilt too. Guilt is personal. We must each accept responsibility for sin and face the guilt associated with it. We cannot blame others for our sins, but are accountable to God personally.

Paul makes a clear case for the sinfulness of humanity, the necessity for God's intervention, and personal accountability for sin in Romans 1:18 to 3:20. All people, says Paul, both Gentiles (Rom. 1:18–32) and Jews (Rom. 2:1 to 3:8) are guilty of sin. All people rebel and are arrogant and idolatrous. All are under the power of sin (Rom. 3:9). According to Paul, we are all ruled by sin and are accountable to God.

Guilt is a concept of such magnitude that we are all mired down in it. There is a sense of shame and responsibility at personal wrongdoing and offenses. Counselors' and ministers' offices are full of people, even Christian people, who are burdened down by guilt. Sometimes we let guilt paralyze us completely. The relationship of guilt and blame to forgiveness is an important concept, which chapters 10 and 11 deal with in more detail.

Spiritual Death

Spiritual death is the most severe consequence of sin. If a person sins continually and consistently and never comes under the lordship of Christ through repentance and faith, she or he will die spiritually. In Romans 6:23, Paul tells us that the wages of sin are death (NIV) or that sin pays off with death (CEV).

Revelation 20:14–15 describes the second death as being in the lake of fire if one's name is not written in the book of life. This is spiritual death in hell. Hebrews 2:14–15 talks about the devil and his power over death. Satan helped instigate sin in the Garden of Evil and he continues to tempt and trick persons to sin today.

Eternal damnation, eternal separation from God, and spiritual death are realities if a person does not accept God's saving grace and mercy. These dire circumstances caused by sin should motivate us as Christ followers to eagerly and actively share the good news about forgiveness and salvation through Jesus Christ.

Separation from God

Sin separates us from God. It brings about an estranged relationship with Him and a lack of fellowship. Adam and Eve experienced this separation, and so do we, when we sin. When a person dies without Christ, the tragedy is a permanent and eternal separation from God and eternal death (Rom. 6:23).

You, like me, probably know this feeling well. When I sin, I am out of fellowship with God or another person until I seek and accept forgiveness. The good news is that this condition does not have to be permanent. Acceptance of Jesus Christ as Lord and Savior brings eternal life and eternal fellowship with God. It does not mean that we will never sin again because sin is our nature. It does mean that we live under God's grace and mercy and for the most part will seek to follow His will. When we do sin again, we can ask forgiveness by confessing our sin, repenting, and being restored into God's fellowship and service.

Interpersonal Problems

Sin not only separates us from God, it is also responsible for all interpersonal problems. Sin creates and feeds the feelings of estrangement from others. This cleavage happens even in the best of relationships, let alone those relationships that are already fragile and fractured.

James 4:1–3 paints a graphic picture of the estrangement sin brings about between people:

"Why do you fight and argue with each other? Isn't it because you are full of selfish desires that fight to control your body? You want something you don't have, and you will do anything you can to get it. You will even kill! But you still cannot get what you want and you won't get it by fighting and arguing. You should pray for it. Yet even when you do pray, your prayers are not answered, because you pray just for selfish reasons."

I must admit that I felt overwhelmed with hopelessness and despair when I finished the research and drafted the two chapters of this book related to sin. The terror of sin and its consequences grieved me beyond end. I was demoralized. Though I know sin is not the end and that there is a better way, it is still a grim, depressing picture.

There is more to the story of God's forgiveness, however. The story does not end with sin or its consequences. There is indeed hope. The remainder of this book explores God's marvelous and wondrous plan of forgiveness and salvation and how it unfolds in our lives today. The second half of Romans 6:23 gives the end of the story as a contrast to the wages of sin being death: "But God's gift is eternal life given by Jesus Christ our Lord." This promise negates the consequences of sin when a person accepts God's gift of forgiveness and eternal life.

Questions for Thought and Discussion

1. How has sin created a barrier between you and God? Identify a time when there was a barrier between you and another person.

2. What does God's intervention in human history mean to you personally?

3. How do you know sin enslaves persons or groups in society? Give some examples. How has sin enslaved you?

4. Where do you see spiritual depravity today? What can you do about it?

5. How are you spiritually blind because of sin? What about treatment of the poor today?

6. How does sin makes persons morally inept today? Do you know anyone like this? In what ways has sin negatively affected your values and standards?

7. Do you ever feel guilty when you sin? How does guilt affect you and what do you do about it?

8. How would you contrast spiritual death and eternal life?

9. How do you feel when estranged from God? Another person? Describe a time when you were estranged from another person, perhaps a significant other. What did this estrangement do to you? How did you react?

---

[1]Trent C. Butler, ed., *Holman Bible Dictionary* (Nashville: Holman Bible Publishers, 1991), 1283.

3

How Did God Forgive Sin in the Old Testament?

The same way He did in the New Testament, except that repentance was expressed through a sacrificial system that pointed to Christ's future atonement.

If you've ever experienced doubt that God can forgive and use a broken vessel, Janie's (not her real name) story should wipe out that doubt. I met, or more accurately encountered, Janie at a women's retreat several years ago.

Early one morning I followed a group of young women from the lodge to the dining room. My eyes were drawn immediately to Janie. In contrast to the other young women, she wore a sleeveless, studded leather jacket covered with badges from "bike" shows (I mean big bikes—motorcycles!), faded jeans, and rough and worn boots. She limped,

Genesis 12:1–3; 15:5–8,18–21; 17:8; 4:2–5; 8:21; 22; 12:10–20; 20:1–18; 12:1–3; 15:1–5; 17:15–22; 18:1–15; 21:1–7; 16:1–6; 25–28; 28–36

Exodus 1–18; 19–40; 2:11–15; 18:13–26; 19:5–6; 6:6; 15:13

Leviticus 4–5

Numbers 11:16–17

Deuteronomy 7:18

Judges 6–8; 13–16

1 Kings 17–19

Ezra

Nehemiah

Psalms 103:13; 25:4–7; 40:11–12; 51:1–4; 23:6; 25:6; 103:17; 117:2; 77:15

Proverbs 28:13–14; 54:7

using a cane, and scars were visible on her arms and face.

My first impression of Janie was definitely not positive. Latent prejudice gushed up in me like bile rising in a person's throat from an acid reflux attack. I broke out in a sweat. *What was she doing at this retreat?* I thought. *Someone from a motorcycle gang?* Since childhood I had seen "those people" as uncouth, big and burly, unshaven, crude, dirty, having a less-than-desirable lifestyle.

Isaiah 1:10–17; 49:15; 54:6–8; 63:15–16; 55:7; 1:10–18; 54:8

Jeremiah 7:1–26; 31:20

Lamentations 3:31–33

Daniel 9:9

Hosea 2:19–20; 6:6

Amos 1:11; 5:21–27

Micah 6:4–6; 7:19

Malachi 1:7–14

Romans 12:1–2

Hebrews 11; 11:23–29; 10:1–4

My assignment at this retreat involved teaching the book *Transformed: Shaped by the Hand of God.* To my chagrin Janie appeared in the first workshop and sat on the front row right in front of me. *OK, Lord,* I uttered silently, *what are You trying to teach me?* Janie was an eager and avid learner and participated energetically in every activity. As the women molded their handful of modeling clay into their concept of God's transformation process, I watched Janie covertly out of the corner of my eye. A beautiful little clay vase took shape in her hands. And, of course, she came to chat with me after the workshop. I could only gulp out meek responses.

During the final service Janie limped to the front and sang a beautiful a cappella contralto solo. Her face was radiant and tears coursed down her cheeks. She looked like someone transformed. I was moved beyond my wildest imagination and felt so very close to God. *OK, Lord, tell me what You are trying to teach me,* I prayed silently.

As we were loading the vans to leave, Janie sought me

out. As she thanked me for my part in the retreat, she gave me the little molded clay vase, this time containing tiny wild flowers she had picked from the grounds around the retreat center. She told me how God had earlier transformed her life. Married to a military man and in the military herself, they had led rough and undesirable lives as they moved from base to base. Janie suffered untold agony from injuries received in a serious bike accident that almost took her life. Though God reached out to her and she responded to Him, Janie despaired of her alcoholic husband who drank himself into a stupor every night. God's grace and her concern for her son were all that kept Janie going. God intervened in her life again, however, when He miraculously saved her husband in his drunken state in a bar. This depraved and sinful man truly found the Lord that night and their lives were transformed.

The woman I had seen as a scarred, broken vessel was indeed God's living vessel. This woman was a living testimony of transformation to those with whom she related—bikers, military personnel, and her community of faith. She was a rock of strength and faith in her church and a mentor to these young women from a remote military base. Did the Lord teach me, another broken vessel, anything that weekend? Oh yes, He taught me in a fresh way about His love and acceptance.

The incredible story of God's plan of forgiveness begins in the Old Testament. Sin entered the world and God progressively unveiled His plan of forgiveness and salvation that culminated in the Cross. Therefore, we begin with the understanding of forgiveness in the Old Testament, grow in our understanding through the New Testament, and ultimately experience forgiveness personally. Though God's grace, mercy, and forgiveness are absolute mysteries to our finite minds, He did and does relate to fallible, sinful human beings as a perfect God.

The Old Testament Story

The Old Testament is about God and His revelation of Himself. God chose to become involved in the life of a small, backwater Hebrew people known as Israel. The sovereign, holy God wanted contact and a relationship with these flawed creatures who discovered sin and disobedience in the Garden of Eden.

Throughout the Old Testament, God kept on pursuing the rebellious Israelites. No matter how far His people fell away, God proved himself time and again as Emmanuel, that is, God with us. He clothed Adam and Eve after their rebellion. He gave the Patriarchs (founding fathers) Abraham, Isaac, and Jacob, the great Exodus leader Moses, the judges, the kings, and the prophets one chance after another. He endured the indignities of Israel's unfaithfulness and responded with even more love.

God revealed himself in the Old Testament as a God of love, grace, mercy, and forgiveness. He cared about His people and gave them His utmost attention. He wanted them to be like Him, to worship Him, and to be in a right relationship with Him. In the Old Testament God set forth His definition of forgiveness as an act of His grace and mercy to forget forever and not hold people of faith accountable for sins they confess.

From the beginning God began to establish covenants or agreements with His people. The first covenant was with Abraham (then called Abram), a man who according to Hebrews 11 was a man of great faith. God chose Abraham to be the father of His new nation, instructing Abraham to leave his country and people and go to a new land. God agreed to give land to Abraham, found a great nation through him and bless it, give Abraham many descendants, and bless all peoples of the earth through this new nation (Gen. 12:1–3; 15:5–8,18–21;

17:8). Abraham's part of the agreement was to obey God. We see unfolded before us the beginning of God's covenant people and the broad outline of His salvation plan. Salvation comes by faith. Abraham's descendants will be God's people. And the Savior of the world will come through this chosen nation. Be assured: God has a plan of forgiveness for all human beings.

Through many experiences God taught Abraham how to live a life of faith. God's covenant continued with Abraham's immediate descendants, who were simple ordinary people like us. Through them God did great things in His kingdom.

God then chose Moses to deliver His people from their harsh taskmasters in Egypt through the Red Sea and into the desert for 40 years. There He developed them as a nation (Ex. 1–18). In a dramatic meeting with Moses on Mount Sinai, God made another covenant with His people, this time about how to live the right way and how to worship Him (Ex. 19–40). The covenant included a sacrificial system through which God granted forgiveness. The people's part of this covenant was to obey God's laws and remain faithful to Him. The people struggled to keep their part of the agreement with God, but He continually offered guidance and forgiveness when they disobeyed Him.

From that point on the children of Israel gained a basic understanding of their own identity and the identity and character of God. God remained faithful to the covenant despite the infidelity of the people. He loved them and they needed to respond to His love.

The remainder of the Old Testament—through the period of the judges, the kings, and the captivity of the Northern and Southern Kingdoms by the Assyrians and Babylonians, is story after story of ordinary people who struggled with issues of faith and obedience and learned how a loving God relates to them. He is a God of forgiveness and forgave the people over and over when they confessed their sins and wrongdoing.

God's Sacrificial System in the Old Testament

What is a sacrifice anyhow? Consider these common examples. Sacrifices are common in the sport of baseball. A batter sometimes hits a sacrifice fly that an outfielder catches, but this allows a runner on the batter's team to score. And often a batter bunts the ball and is put out at first base, while a teammate advances one base. In each case the batter sacrifices the opportunity to get a hit for the larger good of the team. A sacrifice involves giving up something for someone else or for the greater good.

Parents regularly make sacrifices so their children can have or experience certain things. After we moved to Washington, D.C., following World War II, my parents scrimped and saved in order to purchase two hard-to-get tickets for the January 1949 inauguration of Harry S Truman as President of the United States. But these tickets were not for them; they were for my brother and me. My parents could afford only two tickets. They wanted my brother and me to watch the inaugural parade close-up from bleacher seats on Pennsylvania Avenue, an experience far different from watching on our black-and-white television set and one we will never forget. Now, after watching numerous other inaugural parades on TV, I am grateful for this sacrifice on the part of my parents. No doubt you have made many sacrifices for your family or friends, and have done it willingly and gratefully.

Nothing, however, can compare with God's sacrifice. God's plan of salvation and forgiveness involves a sacrificial system, inaugurated in the Old Testament. The primary means of obtaining forgiveness then was through the sacrificial system of the covenant relationship between God and His chosen people, Israel. A sacrifice is "an act of offering to deity something precious; *esp:* the killing of a victim on an altar." It can also mean "destruction or surrender of something for the sake of something else," or "something given up or lost."[1]

The custom of a sacrificial system was not unusual in the ancient Near East and was evident from the beginning of Old Testament times. People of many nations practiced sacrifice as a religious expression. Sacrifice in the Old Testament related to worship. The worshiper brought physical elements—animals, grain, etc.—to God to express devotion, thanksgiving, or the need for forgiveness. The Book of Genesis gives many examples. Cain and Abel, the sons of Adam and Eve, offered sacrifices to God (Gen. 4:2–5). Cain was a farmer who worked the soil, so he offered part of his harvest. Abel, a shepherd, sacrificed some of sheep from his flock. After getting off the ark after the flood that destroyed all the people of the earth except his family, Noah built an altar and offered burnt animal and bird sacrifices to the Lord. The aroma of the burnt offering pleased God (Gen. 8:21).

Perhaps the best known story of sacrifice is that of Abraham's obedience and willingness to follow God's instructions when told to sacrifice Isaac, his only son (Gen. 22). Abraham did not have to go through with the sacrifice, but he was willing and took all the necessary steps up until God intervened and provided a substitute sacrifice.

Though sacrifice had been practiced in the Old Testament in the early days, it really did not appear as an organized system until God delivered the Israelites from Egypt and developed them into a nation in the wilderness. The sacrificial system God set up expressed the dynamics of the sinful human condition and the need for forgiveness. It also taught the people the necessity of dealing with sin and showed that God had provided a way for dealing with sin. Bringing sacrifices showed a sense of need. Laying hands on the sacrifice symbolized the person's identification with the sacrifice, as did the release of the animal's life through sacrificial slaughter. The sacrifice must be unblemished, stressing the holiness of God contrasted with human sinfulness. And God's forgiveness, channeled through a sacrificial offering, was an act of mercy freely bestowed by God, not purchased by the person bringing the offering. All of this is relevant to our New Testament understanding of God's final and perfect sacrifice through Jesus Christ—the sense of need, the slaughter, the unblemished sacrifice, and God's forgiveness.

Sin prevented the Israelites from approaching God directly, so He established priests and the sacrificial system to help the people approach Him. God would forgive the sins of the Israelites if they would offer certain sacrifices administered by the priests on their behalf. The priests were the people's representatives before God.

Sacrifices and offerings became a regular part of Israel's worship system and were a physical expression of their inward devotion to God. We on the other side of New Testament grace often see the Old Testament sacrificial system as complex and cumbersome. But it helps us understand better the significance of what Christ, the ultimate, perfect, and final sacrifice, did for us on the Cross.

Sacrifices, or offerings, in the Old Testament fell into five categories: burnt, grain, peace, sin, and guilt. These sacrifices, both corporate and individual, were used in conjunction with each other. The offerings showed the seriousness of sin and the necessity of dealing with sin. They also demonstrated God's provision of a way for dealing with sin and the importance of bringing one's sins to God for forgiveness. We cannot forgive ourselves. Only God can forgive sin and restore fellowship. Through God's grace and mercy, we are allowed to have a personal relationship with Him. The Israelites in Old Testament times made sacrifices and offerings to please God, thank God, ask for God's blessing, ask for forgiveness, and restore fellowship.

Though the burnt offering described in Leviticus 1 related to payment for sins in general, the sin and guilt offerings were the primary sacrifices related to sin and the need for forgiveness. The sin offering, described in Leviticus 4–5, was required offering for sins that were unintentional. Worshipers made this offering to ask for forgiveness and to be cleansed from the sins. It showed the seriousness of sin and made payment for those that were unintentional. The sacrifice varied according to who committed the sin, that is, the high priest, the whole nation, a tribal leader, or ordinary people. Different kinds of sacrifices were made for different kinds of sins. The purpose of this offering was to restore the sinner to fellowship with God; thus, its primary purpose was restitution.

The guilt offering, described in Leviticus 5, is similar to the sin offering. It was intended to make things right with God when people had cheated Him without meaning to. It was also an attempt to make up for and ask forgiveness for unintentionally destroying property, robbing, or cheating another person.

Offending persons were guilty and responsible to pay for their offense, even if the sin had been unintentional. In the case of robbery the guilty person had to return the stolen property, plus 20 percent more, and provide a ram for sacrifice.

The five offerings that were part of the Old Testament sacrificial system are forerunners of God's perfect sacrifice and offering of the New Testament. Think of the parallels between the Old Testament system and God's final sacrifice. Both the Old and New Testament expressions of God's provision of a sacrificial system involve perfect and complete sacrifices as substitutes for the sins of humanity. The shedding of blood is necessary. And, they are all outward expressions on the part of the sinner of an inner devotion and means of restoring fellowship with God.

The Israelites were not always faithful to obey the laws, sometimes had improper motives, and even offered sacrifices out of habit rather than worship. They tended to ignore faith, confession, and devotion and concentrated instead on the mere act of sacrifice, thinking this would bring forgiveness. They abused the system. Lest we cast stones, we sometimes fall into these same patterns in our worship of God today. Do our ceremonies, worship practices, even our observances of baptism and the Lord's Supper, ever become repetitious? Do we allow our minds to wander while we worship? Do we ever have improper motives? Is worship ever a habit?

Old Testament prophets dealt harshly with the people's concept of sacrifice. They didn't want to do away with the system, but denounced the misuse of it and tied it directly to worship. Isaiah claimed sacrifices were worthless unless accompanied by repentant hearts and obedient lives (Isa. 1:10–17). Micah told the people that God wanted their hearts and lives, not just the physical act of sacrifice (Mic. 6:4–6). Jeremiah condemned the belief that as long as the Temple was in Jerusalem and the people were faithful to perform sacrifices, God would protect them. The symbol, a temple, had to be reflected in a person's life (Jer. 7:1–26). Malachi chastised the people for offering lame and sick animals to God rather than the best, as Levitical law required. By cheating on the sacrifice, the people defiled the altar and despised God (Mal. 1:7–14). God wanted more than the physical performance of meaningless sacrifices. Rather He wanted His people to live right and for their offerings to show the hearts of the worshipers.

We know from the New Testament how important worship is to the concept of sacrifice. Romans 12:1–2 tells us to offer our bodies as living sacrifices as an act of worship to God. *The Message*, a contemporary rendering of the Bible, states the instruction in a clear way for us:

"So here's what I want you to do, God helping you: Take your everyday, ordinary life—your sleeping, eating, going-to-work, and walking-around life—and place it before God as an offering. Embracing what God does for you is the best thing you can do for him. Don't become so well-adjusted to your culture that you fit into it without even thinking. Instead, fix your attention on God. You'll be changed from the inside out. Readily recognize what he wants from you, and quickly respond to it. Unlike the culture around you, always dragging you down to its level of immaturity, God brings the best out of you, develops well-formed maturity in you."

Examples of Forgiveness

The Old Testament contains many examples of forgiveness, both for individuals and for God's chosen people. Because it tells us more about David than any other person in the Old Testament, the next chapter is the story of God's demonstration of forgiveness to David. We find many additional examples with which we can identify, examples of faith with great strengths, yet with sin and weakness. God used each of these people in mighty ways in spite of their weaknesses.

Think about Abraham and Sarah, models of faith and strength who also sometimes struggled with telling the whole the truth, faltered in their belief in God, took matters in their own hands without consulting God, and covered their faults by blaming others. Yet Hebrews 11, the great New Testament faith chapter, has more to say about them than any other faith heroes or heroines. These stalwarts of faith were obedient to God's call to move to a new land that God promised them and to found a new nation that God would bless and which in turn would bless other nations. Even though Abraham and Sarah were old and beyond the age for having children, God gave them a son to carry out His promise of descendants for the new nation. And who can forget the story of God's supreme testing of Abraham and Abraham's model of obedience when he was willing to sacrifice Isaac, his only son.

Abraham and Sarah sinned just like any humans, historical or contemporary. Abraham sometimes distorted the truth when he was under pressure and involved Sarah in the lies. At least two times Abraham and Sarah were guilty of this sin, both times out of fear and to save Abraham's hide. Abraham had taken Sarah to Egypt for food when the crops failed (Gen. 12:10–20). Because Sarah was beautiful and to avoid what he most certainly believed would result in his death, Abraham had Sarah identify herself to the king's officials as his sister. While it was true that Sarah was Abraham's half sister, neither Abraham nor Sarah identified her as his wife. Pharaoh and his officials reaped the consequences of God's wrath in this case.

As Abraham and Sarah moved into the desert, Abraham again claimed Sarah was his sister and did not reveal her as his wife (Gen. 20:1–18). Again, they told the half-truth, half-lie, this time to King Abimelech of Gerar. And again, Abraham was trying to save his own hide because he feared the king would kill him to take Sarah, his beautiful wife.

Sarah fell victim to other temptations. She seemed to have trouble believing God's promises to her, especially

His promise of a son to carry out His covenant (Gen. 12:1–3; 15:1–5; 17:15–22; 18:1–15). She was 90 years old and it seemed highly unlikely, even impossible, that she would have a baby. With God, she learned nothing is impossible. The couple indeed had a son, Isaac, who brought joy and laughter into their lives and carried on the lineage (Gen. 21:1–7).

Sarah also tried to work problems out on her own without consulting God. After God promised a child, but before Isaac's birth, Sarah couldn't wait and took matters into her own hands (Gen. 16:1–6). From her limited view of God's miracles, Sarah may have figured the only way for Abraham to have a son would be through another woman. This was a common practice in that day. Sarah's plan was for Abraham to sleep with Hagar, Sarah's Egyptian maidservant, who would then give Abraham a son. The plan seemed to work beautifully for Hagar did indeed bear Abraham a son, Ishmael. But another sin emerged: covering one's own faults by blaming others. Sarah blamed Abraham. Hagar blamed and despised Sarah. Disharmony prevailed.

Though Abraham and Sarah sinned, they repented and received God's forgiveness. God demonstrated His grace and mercy and continued to use this faithful couple in His service. Their faith affected history dramatically. God used the nation founded by Abraham and Sarah for His own. Their model of faith culminated ultimately in God's incarnation and the birth, life, death, and resurrection of Jesus Christ. The God of forgiveness does indeed respond to faith even in the midst of failure.

Isaac, miracle child of Abraham and Sarah and included in the Hebrews 11 roll call of faith, and his wife, Rebekah, also made mistakes (Gen. 25–28). A protected son of older parents, Isaac was quiet, an unassuming person, who tended to mind his own business. He picked up at least one of Abraham's weaknesses. Isaac, too, tended to lie under pressure. The example of this sin recorded in Scripture sounds like same song, second verse of Abraham's song. When Isaac and Rebekah moved to Gerar, Isaac was afraid someone might kill him to get Rebekah, who was beautiful. He, too, told King Abimelech that Rebekah was his sister and did not identify her as wife.

Rebekah seemed to wield the power in this family. Isaac, on the other hand, would compromise or do anything he had to do in order to avoid confrontations and conflict. Isaac played favorites between his twin sons, alienating Rebekah. He favored Esau, an outdoorsman and hunter, who brought him wild meat, while Rebekah favored Jacob, a shepherd. When her husband was old and blind, Rebekah and Jacob deceived Isaac into giving his deathbed blessing to Jacob instead of Esau, the firstborn of the twins. This act caused hatred between the brothers and even more favoritism by Isaac and Rebekah. Yet God used Isaac in spite of these shortcomings. Isaac had a great gift of faith in God.

Jacob, twin son number two, was the third link in the patriarchal lineage. In spite of his weaknesses, God used the deceptive Jacob (Gen. 28–36). After Jacob fled from home, he experienced life from the other side. Laban, Jacob's father-in-law, tricked Jacob into working for him an extra 7 years. Jacob was prone to accumulate wealth for its own sake. And, when faced with conflict, he tended to rely on his own resources rather than going to God for help.

Finally, the grabber Jacob (even as a baby in the birth process, he had grabbed Esau's heel) grabbed on to the messenger of God by the Jordan River and would not let go. Jacob came to the realization that he had to depend on God. In his final years of life, Jacob had great faith in God and followed God's will when he took his family to Egypt to be with son Joseph and saved from the famine.

Moses was perhaps the greatest Jewish leader of all time. He set in motion the exodus of the Hebrews from Egypt to the edge of the Promised Land. His life story is a remarkable saga of God's intervention in a person's life in miraculous ways to accomplish His plan for His chosen people. The Old Testament books of Exodus, Numbers, and Deuteronomy, as well as Hebrews 11:23–29, identify much about Moses. He was a man who reacted and intervened when there was a need for leadership. God molded and shaped him from a child into a strong, mature leader. For most of his life Moses was faithful and obeyed God. He also stood as a buffer between God and His chosen people, who failed to trust God time and again.

Even with his productive life for God, Moses revealed some flaws. As an Egyptian prince and young adult, Moses seethed as he witnessed an Egyptian guard beat a Hebrew, one of Moses' people. When he thought no one was watching, Moses murdered the Egyptian and hid the body. But someone had seen him. As a result, Moses had to flee Egypt (Ex. 2:11–15).

Moses sometimes failed to recognize and use the talents of others, a trait that could have possibly destroyed his own leadership. He was overwhelmed by his responsibilities and suffered from leadership fatigue. However, Jethro, his father-in-law, encouraged Moses to share the load and use other competent and trustworthy persons to share the leadership load (Ex. 18:13–26; Num. 11:16–17).

Moses was certainly no exception to temptation and sin. Though he was close to God, the almost constant grumbling and complaining by the children of Israel grated on his nerves. The patient and loving God repeatedly sent miracles to help the people survive their time in the desert wilderness. But the people not only complained, they also plotted to get rid of their leaders, Moses and his brother Aaron. Because of their sins, God did not give the people an easy route of travel to the Promised Land. Instead they had to wander in the wilderness for 40 years. In addition, no one over 40 years of age, including Moses, would enter the Promised Land. In short, Moses failed to enter the land flowing with milk and honey because he sinned.

Many other examples of God's forgiveness fill the Old Testament. God used Gideon and Samson as judges in the period between the time the Israelites started to settle in the Promised Land, but before they were united under one king. Though Gideon had faith that placed him in the Hebrews 11 roll call of faith, he made mistakes (Judg. 6–8). He feared that his own limitations would prevent God from working. He collected gold from the Midianites and made a symbol that became an object of worship. He fathered a son through a concubine resulting in tragedy for his family and Israel. And Gideon failed to establish the nation in God's ways. After his death the people went back to idol worship.

Samson, the strong man and judge, had tremendous potential to set Israel free, but he wasted his strength and life (Judg. 13–16). He also succumbed to the sensual wiles of Delilah, the woman he loved. Samson violated his vow as a Nazirite dedicated to God from birth, and often violated God's law. He confided in the wrong people and used his gifts and abilities unwisely. At the end of his life and blind, Samson recognized his dependence on God, rose to the occasion, and did one final act of great valor. Hebrews 11 includes Samson as well.

The Old Testament contrasts the lives of the kings of Israel who lived for God and the majority who refused to be faithful to God. The kings often disobeyed or abandoned God's commands and worshiped other gods. Prophets confronted the kings, issued warnings, and brought reminders of lessons from the past. Even Solomon, David's chosen heir and a great and wise king, sinned. Though Solomon built the Temple in Jerusalem, he is not included in the roll call of faith in Hebrews. He made many foreign agreements by marrying pagan women. He then let his pagan wives affect his loyalty to God. Solomon also taxed the people unmercifully and excessively. God Himself said Solomon did not walk before Him with integrity and uprightness (1 Kings 9:3). However, whenever Solomon and the other kings repented and returned to God, God heard their prayers and forgave them.

Even Elijah, one of the greatest Old Testament prophets and committed to God, exhibited human weakness (1 Kings 17–19). Though he challenged Israel's King Ahab and Queen Jezebel, who followed the Canaanite god Baal, Elijah was faithful to his task but paid the price with isolation and loneliness. Elijah fled in terror from Jezebel when she threatened his life. He was afraid, depressed, and felt abandoned. He struggled with his feelings and lack of faith. But, our faithful and loving God revealed Himself again and again to Elijah and used him to accomplish major miracles.

God is always with His people. He has work for each of us to do even when we are afraid and fail Him. He gives us His resources and relates personally and intimately to us. God forgives and restores His people to usefulness.

What the Old Testament Teaches About Forgiveness

Through His acts of forgiveness described in the Old Testament, God displays His qualities of grace and mercy. The almighty God of the Old Testament forgot sin forever and absolved people of their sin and guilt when they confessed. He brought them back into a right relationship with Him.

I began to understand mercy through the example of my mother. She was the most caring, compassionate, ministering person I have ever known. A model of mercy, she was known for meeting the needs of others, especially in cases of sickness, death, or loneliness, often taking those recovering into her home. She enjoyed taking care of the "widow ladies" and for "tending to the old people," many older than she. Perhaps you have experienced or observed human mercy in action.

Yet nothing compares to God's mercy. His forgiveness, channeled through the sacrificial system in the Old Testament, is an act of mercy freely bestowed. The sinner bringing the offering did not purchase forgiveness; the ever-merciful God granted it freely. God's forgiveness of sins is the ultimate expression of mercy.

The Old Testament often uses family terms when referring to God's love, mercy, and compassion. David compares God's kindness or compassion to the kindness of parents to their children (Psalm 103:13). Jeremiah calls the people of Israel God's children who He wants near Him so He can have mercy on them (Jer. 31:20). Isaiah uses examples of a mother who abandoned an infant (Isa. 49:15), a young and brokenhearted wife divorced by her husband (Isa. 54:6–8), or Israel's plea for mercy and help (Isa. 63:15–16) to show in each case God's mercy and compassion.

The prophet Hosea, ever faithful to a sinful wife, said God would accept Israel as his wife forever, but instead of a bride price, would give "justice, fairness, love, kindness, and faithfulness (Hos. 2:19–20). The prophet Amos used the term *relatives* (Amos 1:11).

Why was God merciful to Israel when the people constantly disobeyed Him and sinned? God had chosen Israel to be His people and had a mission for them. God called Abraham and promised him a nation who would bless all peoples of the earth (Gen. 12:1–3). He miraculously led the children of Israel out of Egypt (Ex.) and provided for them while they were in the wilderness for so long. God constantly delivered His chosen people from their enemies. He refers to Israel as a treasured possession who would be a kingdom of priests and a holy nation (Ex. 19:5–6).

The Old Testament is full of Scriptures illustrative of God's readiness to forgive when people are penitent. In Psalm 25:4–7 the psalmist David calls on God to show him His ways, to teach, to guide, and to remember His great mercy and love. He asks God not to remember the sins of his youth or his rebellious ways, but to show love. In Psalm 40:11–12 David pleads with the Lord not to withhold His mercy, asks for God's love and truth, and acknowledges his troubles, sins, and failing heart. And, in Psalm 51:1–4, David calls for God's mercy according to His unfailing love and great compassion. He asks God to blot out his transgressions, wash away all his iniquity, and cleanse him from his sin. David acknowledges that his sin is against God.

The writer of Proverbs states that whoever confesses and renounces sin finds mercy (28:13–14). Isaiah says that even though God abandoned His people for a brief moment, He brought them back with deep compassion (54:7). And, he calls on the wicked to forsake his way and the evil person his thoughts and turn to God, for God will have mercy and freely pardon (Isa. 55:7). Jeremiah reminds us in Lamentations (3:31–33) of God's compassion and unfailing love.

Daniel says God is merciful and forgiving, even though the people have rebelled against Him (Dan. 9:9). The prophet Micah identifies God as a God Who pardons sin, forgives transgressions, doesn't stay angry forever, shows mercy, has compassion, and will tread sins underfoot and hurl iniquities into the depths of the sea (Mic. 7:19).

God requires only one thing of a person in order to receive His mercy, compassion, and forgiveness: a repentant heart. The prophets make the requirement of a penitent heart clear in the Old Testament. God wants justice, not sacrifices (Isa. 1:10–18). He wants worship. He wants His people to live right and be cleansed. He wants faithfulness and an intimate relationship with His people (Hos. 6:6). And He wants justice and fairness rather than sacrifices (Amos 5:21–27). God does not demand sacrifices, but repentant hearts in order to receive His mercy.

God's Forgiveness Is Permanent and Repeated

According to the Old Testament, God's forgiveness is permanent. David was well aware of the permanence of God's mercy and forgiveness and speaks of it often because he had personally experienced it. Chapter 4 closely examines David's story of sin and forgiveness.

Notice these verses from Psalms that show how David felt about God's forgiveness and its permanence:

- "Your kindness and love will *always* be with me each day of my life, and I will live forever in your house, Lord" (Psalm 23:6, *author's italics*).
- "Please, Lord, remember, you have *always* been patient and kind [mercy and love, NIV]" (Psalm 25:6, *author's italics*).
- "The Lord is *always* kind [the Lord's love, NIV] to those who worship him, and he keeps his promises to their descendants who faithfully obey him" (Psalm 103:17, *author's italics*).
- "His love for us is wonderful; his faithfulness *never ends*" (Psalm 117:2, *author's italics*).

Isaiah expresses sentiments similar to David's in what God said to His people: "For a while, I turned away in furious anger. Now I will have mercy and love you *for-*

ever! I, your protector and Lord, make this promise" (Isa. 54:8, *author's italics*).

Over and over God repeats acts of mercy to the children of Israel. Especially is God's mercy evident as He delivers the Israelites from Egypt. He promises to free them from slavery and to redeem them (Ex. 6:6; 15:13; Deut. 7:8; Psalm 77:15). God also shows His mercy in restoring His people from captivity in Babylon back to their homeland (Ezra; Neh.).

God is forever faithful in reaching out to His people in their need for forgiveness. Because the Old Testament sacrificial system could never give once-for-all forgiveness, the sacrifices had to be repeated over and over (Heb. 10:1–4). And, God's mercy and forgiveness also had to be repeated over and over. However, as often as the Old Testament people repented of their sins and asked for forgiveness, God forgave them.

Questions for Thought and Discussion

1. What do you think of when you hear the word *sacrifice*? Describe some personal experiences of sacrifice or modern stories with which you are familiar.

2. You may be thinking, "What does this have to do with me?" What elements of the Old Testament sacrificial offerings were forerunners of God's final and perfect sacrifice through Jesus Christ? What do these elements mean to you today?

3. What does thanksgiving for God's blessings have to do with forgiveness? For what are you thankful?

4. What do the sin and guilt offerings symbolize to you today? How do you feel the need for forgiveness and to be free from guilt? How do you express these feelings?

5. Describe some examples of mercy, human or divine, you have experienced or observed. What was required in each case?

6. How do you know God's mercy and forgiveness are permanent? What assurances do you have?

7. What is a repentant heart and why is it a requirement for forgiveness? Describe true repentance.

---

[1]*Merriam-Webster's Collegiate Dictionary*, 10th ed., s.v. "sacrifice."

4

Whom Did God Forgive in the Old Testament?

Everyone who repented of sins, confessed them, and trusted God. David's life is a model of human sin and God's forgiveness.

My favorite just-for-fun activity is probably reading. Though I enjoy all kinds of books and magazines, I especially like reading about world and national leaders, both past and present. One man in particular illustrates for me how forgiveness and a forgiving spirit work.

Martin Luther King Jr. was an eloquent Baptist minister and leader of the civil rights movement in the United States from the mid-1950s until his assassination in 1968 at the age of 39. King advocated nonviolent means to achieve civil rights reform and was awarded the Nobel Peace Prize in 1964 for his efforts. Not

Joshua 8–9

1 Samuel 13:14; 13:13–14; 16:12; 16:18; 18; 18:27

1 Samuel 16 to 1 Kings 2:11

2 Samuel 2:4; 5:3; 5:1–5; 1–10; 19:24–30; 7; 11–24; 11–12; 13–18; 18:33; 24:1–9; 24:1; 12:15–23; 13:28–29; 15: 1–15; 16:22; 18:14; 24:10–16; 24:17

1 Kings 1:1 to 2:12; 2:25; 2:2–4

1 Chronicles 21:1; 21:8; 22:1–5; 22:6–10; 22:17–19

2 Chronicles 8:14; 21:7

Psalms 51:2; 51:7; 51:10; 51:5; 51:11–12; 51:14; 32:1; 38; 39; 130

Isaiah 9:7

Jeremiah 33:20–22

only did King believe that nonviolent resistance was a powerful weapon for oppressed people who struggled for freedom, he also had faith that everyone in America, both black and white, would some day attain equal justice.

Matthew 1:1; 6
Luke 1:32
Acts 13:22
Hebrews 11:18–32

King's now famous "I Have a Dream" speech reflects a spirit of forgiveness that challenges us all:

"But there is something that I must say to my people who stand on the warm threshold which leads into the palace of justice. In the process of gaining our rightful place we must not be guilty of wrongful deeds. Let us not seek to satisfy our thirst for freedom by drinking from the cup of bitterness and hatred.

We must forever conduct our struggle on the high plane of dignity and discipline. We must not allow our creative protest to degenerate into physical violence. Again and again we must rise to the majestic heights of meeting physical force with soul force. The marvelous new militancy which has engulfed the Negro community must not lead us to distrust of all white people, for many of our white brothers, as evidenced by their presence here today, have come to realize that their destiny is tied up with our destiny and their freedom is inextricably bound to our freedom. We cannot walk alone."[1]

King clearly knew the relationship between attitude and action, belief and behavior. He knew that it mattered not just what he did in his pursuit of civil rights, but also how he did it. He realized that his words and actions could have consequences that would touch thousands of lives and span decades in history. And he understood that an unforgiving spirit would ultimately hurt not only his cause but his soul as well. Sins of the past did not justify further sins, but in fact called him to a higher plane of living—the plane of forgiveness. And he paid the ultimate sacrifice.

Many people today question whether God's grace, mercy, and forgiveness really work. Are they relevant for today since sin seems so rampant and out of control? Will God truly forgive any sins? And what happens afterwards?

Examples of God's forgiveness abound in Scripture, perhaps none so poignant as in the life of David. David was no ordinary person, but one of high stature, a world leader. The Bible describes him as a man after God's own heart (1 Sam. 13:14; Acts 13:22 NIV). Though he was one of the greatest men in the Old Testament and an outstanding model of leadership both then and now, David was not immune to sin or its consequences. However, when he confessed and repented of his sins, sins that we would consider major and serious, God granted him grace and forgiveness. Read David's incredible story as found in 1 Samuel 16 to 1 Kings 2:11, and catch glimpses of his life and feelings in his psalms.

David's Life

Shepherd, musician, giant-killer, soldier, king, and *poet*—David was all of these. Jesus Christ Himself was of the house and lineage of David (Matt. 1:1, 6; Luke 1:32). In short, David was the greatest king of Israel, the ancestor of Jesus Christ, a man after God's own heart, and included in the great roll call faith (Heb. 11:18–32). Though he was a godly role model, he was also human and a sinner, in need of God's forgiveness.

While Saul was still on the throne and David only a boy, Samuel anointed David as Israel's next king. Samuel was Israel's last judge and God's servant during a transition period in the history of Israel, as the nation moved from the rule of judges to the rule of kings.

God rejected Saul, Israel's first king, because of his disobedience (1 Sam. 13:13–14) and chose David who was from the tribe of Judah in Bethlehem. David was Jesse's eighth and youngest son. Described as a "healthy, good-looking boy with a sparkle in his eyes" (1 Sam. 16:12), David had to be called in from his shepherd duties of tending the sheep after Samuel had rejected the seven other sons.

His anointing done in secret, David began to serve Saul almost immediately. He was not publicly appointed king until much later (2 Sam. 2:4; 5:3). When an evil spirit troubled Saul, David could comfort him by playing his harp. One official described David this way: "He's a brave warrior, he's good-looking, he can speak well, and the Lord is with him" (1 Sam. 16:18). Seeds of discord were sown at that time, however. David had courage in contrast to Saul's fear and anxiety.

Young David then bravely conquered Goliath, the Philistine giant over nine feet tall who had terrorized Saul and his army. Daily Goliath would issue a taunting challenge for Israel to send its best soldier out to fight him. The boy David, wearing no armor, bested the giant with only a slingshot and one smooth rock. After this experience David became one of Saul's soldiers and lifelong best friend of Jonathan, Saul's son (1 Sam. 18).

David's relationship with Saul featured many ups and downs—mostly downs. Saul turned against David, jealous over his success. He plotted against David and tried to have him killed. Saul became David's enemy—a very dangerous one. David had to flee and escaped from Saul time and time again. The story of David and Jonathan during this period provides a beautiful model of friendship (1 Sam. 18–27).

After Saul was killed in battle, David was anointed as king, took the fractured kingdom Saul left behind, and built a strong, united power. He was crowned king over Judah, his own tribe, and then king over all of Israel and Judah (2 Sam. 5:1–5). A successful king, David governed

God's chosen nation by God's principles. He brought the ark of the covenant back to the tabernacle in Jerusalem, led his armies to victory over all their enemies, and completed the conquest of the Promised Land begun by Joshua (Josh. 8–9).

King David's accomplishments were many. He moved the people from tribal independence to a centralized government with Jerusalem as its capital; from the leadership of judges to a monarchy; from decentralized worship to worship in Jerusalem. He was popular with the people and had great influence. He showed justice and mercy to everyone—Saul's family, enemies, rebels, allies, and friends (2 Sam. 1–10). He fulfilled his promise to Jonathan by taking care of Jonathan's grandson Mephibosheth (2 Sam. 19:24–30).

David wanted to build a great temple in which the people could worship God. Instead, God promised David that one of his descendants would always be king and that David's son, not David, would build the temple (2 Sam. 7).

Everything seemed to be going right for David. How could anything be better? David followed God. He ministered to people and became a great warrior. He was a role model par excellence. He accomplished much in his journey from shepherd boy to king over a great nation.

Perhaps life's greatest points and highest moments render us most vulnerable to sin. Godliness does not guarantee an easy and carefree life and immunity from sin. Here David's successes turn to struggles because of his sins.

A Turn for the Worse

Human and sinful by nature, David at times stumbled when tempted and fell into sin. Second Samuel 11–24 describes David's troubles and failures, which could easily label him as a betrayer, liar, adulterer, and murderer.

Just enumerate the sins: intrigue, sexual sins, murder, out-of-control family, disobedience. Three major sins of David emerge in 2 Samuel:
- He committed lust, adultery, and murder.
- He failed to deal decisively with the sins of his children.
- He directly disobeyed God in taking a census of the army.

After restoring Israel to peace and great military power, David's personal life became entangled in sin (see 2 Sam. 11–12). Though the country was strong, David grew weak. It was springtime and David again sent his army out to fight. But this time he remained in Jerusalem. He abandoned his purpose by staying home from war. Perhaps this led to a feeling of boredom and aimlessness. David was ripe for Satan's temptation.

One evening as David strolled on his roof, he saw Bathsheba, a beautiful woman, bathing in her courtyard. Bathsheba was a married woman, the wife of Uriah, one of David's soldiers. David, also married, was filled with lust. He had Bathsheba brought to him. David sinned, committing adultery with Bathsheba. After all, he was the king and could have anything or anyone he wanted.

The situation intensified and David fell even more deeply into sin. When David discovered Bathsheba was pregnant, he panicked and plotted. He tried to cover up his sin. First, David tried to arrange matters so it would appear the baby was Uriah's. But Uriah did not cooperate because of his soldierly duties. Then David sent Uriah off to battle, with instructions that he be placed on the front lines, where he would be killed. To lust and adultery, David added the sin of murder.

As soon as possible, David married Bathsheba. She moved into the palace and their son was born. But all was not well, as we will see later in this chapter. David reaped the consequences of these sins and suffered the ruination of his family and the nation.

52
Chips Off the Old Block

David experienced trouble and distress, both with his family and the nation, as a consequence of his sins and cover-up with Bathsheba. Violence tore his family apart and David did not deal decisively with the sins of his children. Again he showed a lack of character in personal decisions (see 2 Sam. 13–18).

What happened with David's family? Amnon, one of David's sons, disgraced Tamar, his half sister. Amnon fell in love with Tamar, a virgin, and raped her, violating any chance she had of a suitable marriage with another royal family. Amnon's so-called love turned to lust and finally hatred. David was furious with Amnon for raping Tamar, but David did not punish him.

The family saga only worsened. Absalom, Tamar's full brother, responded to Tamar's desolate situation and took her into his home. Two years later, Absalom took matters into his own hands and acted on his intentions from the day Amnon raped Tamar. Absalom murdered his half brother. Because of his sin, Absalom fled and stayed away from Jerusalem for 3 years. David's heart longed for Absalom and eventually David let Absalom return home. It was 2 years before they saw one another and were reconciled.

Absalom was a handsome, independent, scheming young man who was impetuous and acted on his own. Apparently David favored him and made no attempt to discipline him. Absalom continued to do whatever he wanted, even conspiring against David and inciting the nation to rebel. He tried to undermine his father David by winning the favor of the northern tribes and had himself crowned king.

David was forced to flee from Jerusalem. Absalom was accidentally killed in a battle between his soldiers and David's soldiers in Ephraim Forest. Devastated when he heard the news of Absalom's death, David wept and cried: "My son Absalom! My son, my son Absalom! I wish I could have died instead of you! Absalom, my son, my son!" (2 Sam. 18:33).

David eventually returned to Jerusalem and tried to reunite Israel and Judah, but the damage was done. He restored the kingdom, but hints of division remained.

An Unwise Decision

Though Bible scholars hold differing opinions about this episode, it may have happened in the prime of David's life. David deliberately sinned against God by taking a census of the soldiers. Apparently he was making some changes in the ways Israel secured its army (see 2 Sam. 24:1–9; 1 Chron. 21:1).

During the period of the judges, Israel was only loosely organized and each tribe was virtually independent. Each tribe mustered its own troops for defense purposes. It was not unusual for a tribe to refuse to provide troops in an emergency if the national emergency was far away from home. Saul, the first king of Israel, did not change this practice.

External pressures were more prevalent during David's reign than during Saul's. David strengthened the central government, depended heavily on his army, and sought better ways to ensure a professional standing army. He also proposed reorganizing the tribal militia, which necessitated taking a census. The perception was that he would follow up with a draft or conscription.[2]

In this instance Joab, David's commander, was wise. He urged David not to take the census because of the expected reaction of the people. They would object to a draft, conscription, or increased taxes. Joab also believed God would provide soldiers. David did not listen to Joab's advice, nor did he change his mind. He took the census, a process that took nine months.

Why was taking a census a sin? Leaders had counted the Israelites in the past, but only when God told them to do so. There is some confusion about the meaning of 2 Samuel 24:1 and 1 Chronicles 21:1 and who told David to take the census. The 2 Samuel account attributed the motivation for David's act to God's anger. For some reason it appeared that God was so angry with Israel that He incited David to take the census so God could vent His wrath. The 1 Chronicles account, on the other hand, attributed the act to Satan. Most scholars agree that Satan was the instigator.[3]

Nevertheless, the action was an irrational decision on David's part and apparently wrong. God could and did provide for Israel, including an army. It was not up to David. Perhaps David's pride and ambition got in the way of his better judgment.

You Are the Man!

David's sins resulted in confrontation with God and lifelong consequences. God was angry when David committed his sins with Bathsheba. He sent Nathan, a prophet, to deal with David and let him know what his punishment would be. Nathan got David to confess his guilt by first telling him a story about two men, one rich and one poor, who lived in the same town. The rich man had lots of sheep and cows; the poor man had only one little lamb that had become a pet for his children. The rich man had company. Rather than kill an animal from his herd, he stole the poor man's lamb and had it slaughtered.

David was incensed at the rich man's actions and claimed such a man should die. Nathan's indictment of David was pointed: "You are the man." He then pronounced God's judgment on David. Because David disobeyed God and took Uriah's wife for himself, his family would never live in peace. Murder was a constant threat in David's own family. His household would rebel. And his wives would be given to others in public view.

David suffered the consequences of his actions. Even as David pleaded with God, the baby of his illicit relationship with Bathsheba died (2 Sam. 12:15–23). Three of David's sons died violent deaths. His son Absalom attempted to steal the throne and slept openly with David's wives (2 Sam. 13:28–29; 15:1–15; 16:22; 18:14; 1 Kings 2:25).

When David sinned by taking the census, God again confronted him, this time through the prophet Gad. Gad offered David God's three options of punishment: three years of famine, three months of fleeing enemies in pursuit of him, or three days of horrible disease in the land. Though each of the choices was terrible, David chose the disease because God rather than men controlled this punishment. God sent the punishment and 70,000 people died (2 Sam. 24:10–16).

From Sorrow to Joy

Was David sorry for his sins? We know he was because he confessed, repented, and worshiped God. When David's first son by Bathsheba was very ill, David fasted to show his sorrow. He begged God to let the child live. He was desperate and his subordinates feared suicide. After the child died in seven days, however, David cleaned himself up, worshiped the Lord, ended his fast, and comforted Bathsheba (2 Sam. 12:15–23). Perhaps in a sense he was released and returned to life in a more normal fashion.

After the census and God's punishment, David acknowledged that he had sinned terribly and that the people who were punished had done nothing wrong. He asked God to punish him and his family instead of the people (2 Sam. 24:17).

David knew that confession and repentance were essential for forgiveness (1 Chron. 21:8). Some of the psalms he wrote reflect how he poured out his soul to God. David penned Psalm 51, a prayer for forgiveness, after Nathan came to him following his adultery with Bathsheba.

Graphically David expressed the terrible condition of the unforgiven sinner: "Wash me clean from all of my sin and guilt" (Psalm 51:2). "Wash me with hyssop[4] until I am clean and whiter than snow" (Psalm 51:7). "Create pure thoughts in me and make me faithful again" (Psalm 51:10). He acknowledged that he was sinful by his very nature. "I have sinned and done wrong since the day I was born" (Psalm 51:5).

David clearly expressed his grief and sorrow at being separated from God. "Let me be happy and joyful! You crushed my bones, now let them celebrate" (Psalm 51:8). "Don't chase me away from you or take your Holy Spirit away from me. Make me as happy as you did when you saved me; make me want to obey!" (Psalm 51:11–12). And he expressed his guilt. "Keep me from any deadly sin. Only you can save me! Then I will shout and sing about your power to save" (Psalm 51:14).

David pleaded for mercy, forgiveness, and cleansing. He acknowledged that he had sinned against God. Because of David's sins, a man was murdered and a baby died. The sin, however, was ultimately rebellion against God. David asked God to restore the joy of his salvation and make him want to obey. Then he would serve God by teaching others God's laws so they, too, would return to God. David had faith in God. He was honest in acknowledging the seriousness of his sin. He prayed, asking for forgiveness. He was brokenhearted over his sin and confessed his wrongdoing. He repented.

In Psalm 32, a sequel to Psalm 51, David expressed the joy that comes from true forgiveness. Only when a person asks God to forgive sins does God grant real happiness and relief from guilt. In his book *A Faith That Sings*, Paul W. Powell said David was blessed, that is, incredibly happy. His sins had been lifted, taken away, hidden, and canceled.[5] "Our God, you bless everyone whose sins you forgive and wipe away" (Psalm 32:1). Other psalms of David about confession and forgiveness include Psalms 38, 39, and 130.

David's response to his sins and God's confrontation tell us a lot about David. His belief in the faithful and forgiving nature of God was unchangeable. He was quick to confess his sins from his heart, and his repentance was genuine. David never took God's forgiveness lightly or God's blessings for granted. He experienced the joy of forgiveness even when he had to suffer the consequences. While David sinned greatly, he did not sin repeatedly. He learned from his mistakes because he accepted the sufferings they brought.

After God's Own Heart

When David confessed his sins out of a genuine heart of repentance and received God's forgiveness, God restored fellowship and peace between them. Reconciliation with God brought David great joy. He was still a man after God's own heart, he was still the ancestor of Jesus Christ, and his name was recorded in Hebrews 11, the great chapter of faith. The leader David, the sinner David, and the forgiven David had wonderful qualities. He was faithful, patient, courageous, generous, committed, honest, modest, and penitent. Rather than remembering him for his sins, we should instead remember his relationship with God and his ability to confess, repent, accept forgiveness, and live a life that blessed others.

David could have buried his name in shame, but he did not, nor did he give up when intrigue continued in his family. When he was an old man, his son Adonijah sought to inherit the throne. Nathan and Bathsheba worked to ensure that Solomon would be king (1 Kings 1:1 to 2:12).

God's forgiveness restored David's life and service. Though told that Solomon would build the temple rather than himself, David poured himself into making extensive advance preparations for the building and worship services. Even when Solomon was still young, David gathered laborers to work. He stockpiled supplies—stone, iron, bronze, and cedar (1 Chron. 22:1–5).

At the end of his life, David charged his son Solomon to fulfill the promise God had made to him.

"I want you to be strong and brave. Do what the Lord your God commands and follow his teachings. Obey everything written in the Law of Moses. Then you will be a success, no matter what you do or where you go. You and your descendants must always faithfully obey the Lord. If you do, he will keep the solemn promise he made to me that someone from our family will always be king of Israel" (1 Kings 2:2–4).

David told Solomon that his failure to build the temple was due to the shedding of blood. Solomon instead was a man of peace and David prayed for wisdom for him (1 Chron. 22:6–10).

David also encouraged and challenged the leaders, basically telling them not to worry about safety but devote their energies to a constructive project.

"David then gave orders for the leaders of Israel to help Solomon. David said: 'The Lord our God has helped me defeat all the people who lived here before us, and he has given you peace from all your enemies. Now this land belongs to the Lord and his people. Obey the Lord your God with your heart and soul. Begin work on the temple to honor him, so that the sacred chest and the things used for worship can be kept there'" (1 Chron. 22:17–19).

David's legacy is formidable, at least four things making it so. First, he was a role model for Israelite kings. As you read the history of the kings in the books of Kings and Chronicles, you will often see them compared to David. Second, David was a man of God and worshiped the Lord with all his heart, soul, mind, and strength (2 Chron. 8:14) Third, David's life influenced God's decisions about David's disobedient successors (2 Chron. 21:7). And, finally, God's promise to David was fulfilled. David's kingdom did indeed go on forever, for there was a future David—Jesus Christ (Isa. 9:7; Jer. 33:20–22).

David's experiences hold many lessons for twenty-first-century women and men. David was willing to honestly admit his mistakes, the first step in dealing with personal sin. Forgiveness does not remove the consequences of sin. However, God greatly desires our complete trust and worship in spite of sin's consequences. God is faithful always in reaching out to us, restoring relationship and fellowship, and using us in His service.

Questions for Thought and Discussion

1. What qualities did David possess that prepared him to be a future king? What qualities from your childhood and youth have prepared you to serve God?

2. What do you think were David's greatest triumphs and best qualities as a leader? What were his worse qualities? What qualities do you look for in a leader today?

3. What was the significance of God's promise that one of David's descendants would always be king? How does this promise affect you personally?

4. What did David do wrong? How did he make it

worse? When are you most vulnerable to sin? What recourse do you have?

5. Why did God continue to forgive David? Why does he continue to forgive you? What does this tell you about God?

6. Has God ever confronted you about a sin? How did you feel?

7. What do you do when you have sinned?

8. Why are confession and repentance important? What do they mean to you? How do you best express them? What does forgiveness mean to you?

9. What do you consider to be David's legacy? What lessons have you learned from his life, his sins, God's reaction and forgiveness, and David's response?

---

[1] Martin Luther King Jr., "I Have a Dream," speech delivered on the steps of the Lincoln Memorial in Washington, D.C., August 28, 1963.
[2] Clifton J. Allen, ed., *The Broadman Bible Commentary* (Nashville: Broadman Press, 1970), 3:143–44.
[3] Ibid.; Joe O. Lewis, *Layman's Bible Book Commentary* (Nashville: Broadman Press, 1980), 5:123–24.
[4] A small bush with bunches of small, white flowers used to sprinkle blood or water in various ceremonies. *The Learning Bible*, Contemporary English Version (New York: American Bible Society, 2000), 1046.
[5] Paul W. Powell, *A Faith That Sings* (Nashville: Broadman Press, 19__), 62–64.

5

What Difference Did Jesus' Life Make in Forgiveness?

Jesus actually atoned for all humanity's sins—past, present, and future—in the sacrifice of His sinless life.

One of my work responsibilities was to coordinate annual summer events at national conference centers, and, several times a once-every-5-years convention for youth. Through the years I was involved in securing hundreds of speakers and workshop leaders. It was always important to find the right people for the assignments. However, on two occasions, it was absolutely critical. No one else would do.

One summer we held our first-ever special women's weekend event. Our goal was to reach younger women who were not already involved in missions activities, as were the women's missions advocates we had been

Exodus 24:6–8

Isaiah 53

Matthew 28:16:20

Mark 2:1–12; 14:24; 16:15; 1:15; 8:34–37

Luke 3:23; 5:31–32; 9:21–22; 9:44–45; 5:32; 24:47; 13:1–5

John 1:1–18; 8:2–11; 3:16

Acts 13:38–39; 1:8

Romans 3:25–26; 12:1–2; 3:25; 10:9–10; 12:1–2

2 Corinthians 5:17–21

Ephesians 1:4; 2:14–16

Philippians 2:6–11

1 Timothy 2:5

Hebrews 10:1–4; 10:10–14; 4:14 to 5:10; 4:14–16; 5:4–6; 9:14

1 Peter 2:5

1 John 1:9

reaching for years. The worship leader at this event would function as the glue that held the entire experience together, so it was essential that we find just the right person. She had to be a competent musician and a dynamic, committed woman who would appeal to the young women we were trying to influence. She also had to understand the vision for the weekend and the purpose for the experience. We had to find the one and only right person for this assignment.

When we began planning a huge youth event for 1998, we had to find just the right called and committed young woman to lead out in this event, which would attract thousands of teenaged girls. Not just anyone would do. It was critical that this person be just the right person.

Jesus Christ was God's perfect and final sacrifice. No one else would do for God's plan of salvation and experience. *No One* else would do. Only Jesus Christ could carry out this mission.

God's provision of a sacrificial system in the Old Testament was merely a shadow of His perfect and final sacrifice through Jesus Christ. The Old Testament system could never give once-for-all forgiveness. The people had to repeat these sacrifices over and over, year after year. According to Hebrews 10:1–4, the offering of sacrifices on the Day of Atonement only reminded the people of their sins. Animal sacrifices could never take away sins. The Old Testament sacrifices were only a temporary way to deal with sin and guilt.

People needed permanent forgiveness that would destroy their sins forever. The Old Testament sacrificial system gave them a way to make their sacrifices in faith that God would forgive. And, of course, God did. This system pointed to a new way of sacrifice expressed through the New Testament. God provided a perfect and final sacrifice through Jesus Christ, which made it possible for people to confess their sins to God, repent, accept Jesus Christ as Savior and Lord, and be forgiven (1 John 1:9).

The Final Sacrifice

Jesus Christ is the intermediary through which God provides forgiveness for every person and direct access to God. Romans 3:25–26 makes this message clear.

"God sent Christ to be our sacrifice. Christ offered his life's blood, so that by faith in him we could come to God. And God did this to show that in the past he was right to be patient and forgive sinners. This also shows that God is right when he accepts people who have faith in Jesus."

Jesus became the High Priest Who offered for all time one sacrifice for sins.

"So we are made holy because Christ obeyed God and offered himself once for all. The priests do their work each day, and they keep on offering sacrifices that can never take away sins. But Christ offered himself as a sacrifice that is good forever. Now he is sitting at God's right side, and he will stay there until his enemies are put under his power. By his one sacrifice he has forever set free from sin the people he brings to God" (Heb. 10:10–14).

God's plan is wondrous, incredible, beyond belief. How does this plan work? God became incarnate, or took on a human form through His Son Jesus (John 1:1–18). Jesus was conceived miraculously through the power of the Holy Spirit, born to a virgin mother in humble surroundings in Bethlehem. Reread the Christmas story as told in the early chapters of Matthew and Luke. Jesus was human *and* divine, the Son of man and the Son of God. He presents the clearest picture of God the world has ever seen or known. He is God's eternal Son.

Jesus' earthly ministry began when He was about 30 years old and lasted for 3 years (Luke 3:23). In obedience to God, Jesus lived a sinless life and did His Father's will. He taught in the synagogues and other places, preached the good news of God's kingdom, and healed all kinds of sickness and disease. He associated with sinners, for He had come to call them to repentance (Luke 5:31–32). He gathered around him a group of 12 disciples whom He trained and prepared to carry on His mission after His death. The disciples did not really understand what Jesus had come to do, but He tried several times to tell them of His coming death (Luke 9:21–22; 9:44–45).

The religious leaders confronted and threatened Jesus over and over during His public ministry. He was not popular with the religious elite. With His impending death on the Cross constantly on His mind, He steadfastly moved toward His final days in Jerusalem where He knew He would become the final and perfect sacrifice for sin. Jesus intended to fulfill His mission and God's plan that led to His death and resurrection.

All four Gospels (Matthew, Mark, Luke, and John) portray Jesus as the perfect man offered as the perfect sacrifice for the sin of all humanity. Jesus fulfilled God's demand for atonement for sin. He suffered an agonizing death on the Cross, and provided salvation and a way of forgiveness for all humanity (Eph. 1:4). Jesus brought hope to sinners, provided redemption from sin, and restored fellowship with God.

"Christ was truly God. But he did not try to remain equal with God. He gave up everything and became a slave, when he became like one of us. Christ was humble. He obeyed God and even died on a cross. Then God gave Christ the highest place and honored his name above all others. So at the name of Jesus everyone will bow down,

those in heaven, on earth, and under the earth. And to the glory of God the Father everyone will openly agree, 'Jesus Christ is Lord!'" (Phil. 2:6–11).

Crucifixion, the method the Romans used to execute Jesus, was the most painful and degrading form of capital punishment used during that day. The excruciating death on the Cross was the means by which Jesus became the atoning sacrifice for the sins of humanity. It was a vicarious death because Jesus was sinless, but died for the sins of all people of all time.

According to the Old Testament, only God could forgive sin. But Jesus declared He could do so on several occasions, and He did (Mark 2:1–12; John 8:2–11). With His intimate disciples, He spoke of His death as "my blood of the covenant which is poured out for many" (Mark 14:24 NIV). Jesus clearly understood what He was to do.

The Old Covenant involved forgiveness of sins through the blood of animal sacrifice (Ex. 24:6–8). Instead of a spotless lamb on the altar, Jesus offered Himself, the spotless Lamb of God, as a sacrifice that would forgive sin once and for all. Jesus was the final sacrifice for sins, His blood sealing the New Covenant with God so that all people can come to God for forgiveness and salvation through Him.

Jesus fulfilled the Old Testament sacrificial system. He Himself became the Suffering Servant, the unblemished sacrifice, and the bearer of the sins of all humanity described so beautifully in Isaiah 53. Often referred to as the Suffering Servant, this prophecy is the basis for a portion of Handel's *Messiah*. God saved the world through a humble, suffering servant; a man of sorrow, acquainted with grief, despised, and rejected. Nevertheless, Jesus triumphed over death and is now again at the right hand of God.

A New High Priest

The Old Testament presented a wonderful example of true worship and devotion to God. The commandments, rituals, and prophets described God's promises and pointed the way to forgiveness and salvation. Then Jesus came, fulfilling the Law and the prophecy, breaking down all barriers to God, and providing eternal life forever.

A profound account of how New Testament Christianity differs from the religion of the Old Testament lies in the Book of Hebrews. It for all time shows that Jesus is superior and supreme, greater than the angels, greater than Moses, and greater than the Old Testament priesthood. Jesus Christ is the perfect revelation of God, the final and complete sacrifice for sin, the perfect mediator, and the only way to eternal life.

From Hebrews, especially chapters 4:14 to 5:10, we understand that Jesus became the great High Priest. In the Old Testament the high priest was the highest religious authority figure. He alone entered the Holy of Holies in the temple once a year on the Day of Atonement to make atonement for the sins of the people (Lev. 16). The moment Jesus died on the Cross, the great veil in the temple that separated the Holy of Holies from the rest of the sanctuary was torn from top to bottom. At that moment, God opened up direct access to Himself through Jesus Christ.

When Jesus became God's final and perfect sacrifice, He also became the final and only High Priest.

"We have a great high priest, who has gone into heaven, and he is Jesus the Son of God. That is why we must hold on to what we have said about him. Jesus understands every weakness of ours, because he was tempted in every way that we are. But he did not sin! So whenever we are in need, we should come bravely before the throne of our merciful God. There we will be treated with unde-

served kindness, and we will find help. . . . But no one can have the honor of being a high priest simply by wanting to be one. Only God can choose a priest, and God is the one who chose Aaron. That is how it was with Christ. He became a high priest, but not just because he wanted the honor of being one. It was God who told him, 'You are my Son, because today I have become your Father!' In another place, God says, 'You are a priest forever just like Melchizedek'" (Heb. 4:14–16; 5:4–6).

Paul also affirms this concept in his letter to Timothy. *"There is only one God, and Christ Jesus is the only one who can bring us to God. Jesus was truly human, and he gave himself to rescue all of us. God showed us this at the right time" (1 Tim. 2:5).*

Like a high priest, Jesus is a mediator between God and people. As the representative of humanity, He intercedes for us before God. As the representative of God, He assures us of God's forgiveness. He is both God and man. Unlike the Old Testament high priest who could go before God only once a year, Christ is always at God's right hand interceding for human beings. He always hears us when we pray.

The Priesthood of the Believer

A basic doctrine of the Christian faith is the priesthood of the believer, a doctrine especially cherished by Baptists. This doctrine asserts that every individual has direct access to God with no mediator other than Jesus Christ. Christ broke down all barriers (Eph. 2:14–16).

Christ followers can respond directly to God's activity in their lives as He leads through the Holy Spirit and His written Word. They do not need a human priest or minister to be the go-between. Believers are a "holy priesthood" (1 Peter 2:5) and can minister to one another and to the world. "And now you are living stones that are being used to build a spiritual house. You are also a group of holy priests, and with the help of Jesus Christ you will offer sacrifices that please God" (1 Peter 2:5). As living stones, believers offer "spiritual sacrifices" to God through Jesus Christ (Rom. 12:1–2). The sacrifice of self is the Christ follower's response in love and gratitude to God for what He has done for us.

In his article on the priesthood of the believer in the *Holman Bible Dictionary*, Wayne Ward traces the biblical progression of sacrifice. In the Old Testament, the priests sacrificed the animals on the altar. In the New Testament, Jesus became High Priest and offered His own life on the altar of the Cross. Now God calls on believers to be living sacrifices with a day-to-day commitment to do His will and serve Him.[1]

Winds and trends in more recent times have tended to minimize the doctrine of the priesthood of the believer and instead lift up the authority of the clergy or male leadership in the church. I will never forget my shock during a Sunday School class a number of years ago, before this issue raged as much as it does today. The teacher, a woman whom I admired and respected, expounded on "the way to God" being through a man, preferably one's husband. According to her viewpoint, this was biblical. Being single at the time and not agreeing with her anyhow, I tuned out and began to think about other things more important to me.

She, however, was aware of my silent disagreement with her. Perhaps my body language or demeanor betrayed me. She telephoned me that afternoon and began the conversation by asking, "You didn't agree with me this morning, did you?" I flippantly asked her what one did without a husband. She assured me that another male would do and reminded me that I was fortunate enough to have a father in the church. The basic point of discussion, however, was my belief in the doctrine of the priesthood of the believer. I believed then and continue to believe that I have direct access to God through Jesus Christ.

God's Extraordinary Gift

The great God of love, grace, mercy, and forgiveness wants everyone to be saved from her or his sins. God became incarnate, came to earth, and lived among people as God the Son through Jesus Christ. God loved humanity so much He was willing to sacrifice His only Son. "God loved the people of this world so much that he gave his only Son, so that everyone who has faith in him will have eternal life and never really die" (John 3:16). This was the highest price God could pay and the greatest sacrifice He could make. It was truly a work of His grace and mercy.

God offers Jesus as an unblemished sacrifice once for all for the sins of humanity.

- *"But Christ was sinless, and he offered himself as an eternal and spiritual sacrifice to God. That's why his blood is much more powerful and makes our consciences clear. Now we can serve the living God and no longer do things that lead to death"* (Heb. 9:14).
- *"God sent Christ to be our sacrifice. Christ offered his life's blood, so that by faith in him we could come to God. And God did this to show that in the past he was right to be patient and forgive sinners. This also shows that God is right when he accepts people who have faith in Jesus"* (Rom. 3:25).
- *"My friends, the message is that Jesus can forgive your sins! The Law of Moses could not set you free from all your sins. But everyone who has faith in Jesus is set free"* (Acts 13:38–39).

God's plan for salvation and forgiveness is not only eternal but is also universal. His forgiveness is for anyone who truly confesses, repents, and accepts Jesus as Savior:

"whoever believes in him," as John 3:16 says. Jesus came to seek and to save the lost (Luke 5:32). The Great Commissions instructs Christ followers to go to "all nations," "all creation," and "to the uttermost parts of the earth" with the gospel (Matt. 28:16–20; Mark 16:15, Luke 24:47; Acts 1:8).

When God forgives, He never again holds the sins against us. He restores fellowship and relationship with the sinner. The Creator and Author of salvation and forgiveness is the only One Who can forgive sins. He provides a perfect plan of redemption.

Conditions for Forgiveness

God wants to forgive people, His supreme creation. He allowed His beloved Son to die an excruciating and agonizing death just so He could offer pardon and forgiveness. First John 1:9 gives the basic plan for how forgiveness works. "But if we confess our sins to God, he can always be trusted to forgive us and take our sins away." Admitting our sins and confessing them to God is the first step toward forgiveness.

Paul ties confession and belief together in Romans 10:9–10: "So you will be saved, if you honestly say, 'Jesus is Lord,' and if you believe with all your heart that God raised him from death. God will accept you and save you, if you truly believe this and tell it to others." Not only must we confess, we must also repent. Repentance indicates a change of one's heart, a feeling of regret, and a turning away from sin to God. Jesus Himself preached a message of repentance (Mark 1:15; Luke 13:1–5). Repentance involves faith, along with a rejection of sin and a positive response to God. Repentance is a genuine turning from sin toward God. Faith is the acceptance of Jesus Christ and the commitment of one's entire self to Him as Savior and Lord.

When a person receives and accepts forgiveness, she or he is a new person. God has reconciled the individual to Him through Jesus Christ. He has also given the person the ministry of reconciliation, bringing other persons to Him.

"Anyone who belongs to Christ is a new person. The past is forgotten, and everything is new. God has done it all! He sent Christ to make peace between himself and us, and he has given us the work of making peace between himself and others. What we mean is that God was in Christ, offering peace and forgiveness to the people of this world. And he has given us the work of sharing his message about peace. We were sent to speak for Christ, and God is begging you to listen to our message. We speak for Christ and sincerely ask you to make peace with God. Christ never sinned! But God treated him as a sinner, so that Christ could make us acceptable to God" (2 Cor. 5:17–21).

At the point of our salvation we receive the responsibility of living for God and sharing the message of His peace with others.

Questions for Thought and Discussion

1. How would you describe God's plan of salvation and forgiveness to an unbeliever?

2. How does God's provision of a final and perfect sacrifice compare with the Old Testament system described in chapter 3?

3. How did Jesus' earthly ministry indicate that He understood His mission? How did it prepare Him for His final earthly assignment, which was on the Cross?

4. How does God's final and perfect sacrifice change your life? When? What evidences of change do you see?

5. How does Jesus' role as the great High Priest differ from that of the Old Testament priests?

6. How is a twenty-first-century Christ follower expected to sacrifice today? What do Romans 12:1–2 and Mark 8:34–37 say to you about how you should live?

7. What does the doctrine of the priesthood of the believer mean to you? How do you exercise this privilege and responsibility?

8. How would you explain God's role in sacrifice and forgiveness?

9. Explain the conditions for forgiveness. Which comes first, confession or repentance?

10. What does being a "new creature" mean to you? How do you share the gospel of peace with persons with whom you come in contact? To the uttermost parts of the world?

---

[1]Trent C. Butler, ed., *Holman Bible Dictionary* (Nashville: Holman Bible Publishers, 1991), 1137.

6

What Did Jesus Teach About Forgiveness?

He taught that the way to forgiveness is personal repentance and personal forgiveness of others.

Sometimes we make pious platitudes or pronouncements about what we consider right or wrong or what we will or will not do. That, of course, is usually before we are faced with situations that put our pronouncements to the test.

At a conference for which I was responsible, one of the workshop leaders asked if we could talk. I had worked with her closely over the years and considered her a friend, so I felt honored. I could tell by her tone of voice and demeanor that whatever she wanted to discuss was a serious matter.

As we sat on the balcony of my lodge, this qualified and professional woman poured out her heart and soul to me about her family. One daughter, a teenager, was into a wild and undesirable lifestyle that brought agony and grief to her parents. She often disappeared from

Leviticus 20:10

Deuteronomy 22:22–24

Matthew 24–25; 5–7; 6:5–15; 6:12; 6:14–15; 7:1; 7:5; 18:21–35; 18:21; 18:22; 18:26; 18:29; 18:32–33; 18:35; 12:22–32; 12:30–32

Mark 11:25; 3:28–29

Luke 6:17–49; 6:37; 15:3–7; 15:11–32; 15:8–10; 12:8–12; 12:8–10

John 21:25; 14–17; 8; 8:7; 8:10–11

home without notice for weeks at a time. Finally she moved out. The woman and her husband were frantic with worry and concern.

The girl had recently contacted her parents with devastating news. Because of a series of poor choices and bad decisions, she faced a difficult moral dilemma that would forever change her future. Regardless of her subsequent decisions, her parents faced even more grief and would likely be stripped of leadership positions and service opportunities. Yet they knew they must support their daughter with forgiveness, love, and compassion, regardless of what others thought.

"What would you do?" the woman asked me. All the pious platitudes and pronouncements left one by one as my heart flooded with compassion for this woman and her daughter. Dare I cast a stone? What if this was a member of my family? Jesus' teachings about compassion and forgiveness took on a new meaning for me that day as I watched my friend struggle with applying those teachings to her family.

Though Jesus lived only into His 30s and had a fairly short 3-year public ministry, the four Gospels provide us with a fairly comprehensive collection of His teachings. Yet even the Gospel writers offer us only a glimpse of the great wealth of Jesus' teaching ministry. In his Gospel, John wrote that if everything Jesus did was recorded in books, there would not be room enough in the whole world for the books (John 21:25). Using object lessons, lectures, questions, stories, and discussions, Jesus taught significant principles about forgiveness in a variety of ways.

The Sermon on the Mount

Sometimes Jesus lectured or made a more formal presentation in which He did all of the talking. He used this method often in the early part of His ministry, especially when the crowd was unusually large. With no podium or audiovisual system and only a boat or a seat on the hillside, His auditorium was usually by the lake under the sky.

Many of Jesus' sermons are recorded in the Scriptures, but three are especially important: the sermon about the last judgment (Matt. 24–25), the Sermon on the Mount (Matt. 5–7), and Jesus' farewell address (John 14–17). In the Sermon on the Mount Jesus spelled out qualities of a kingdom citizen—what He is looking for in His followers.[1] The sermon includes one important teaching about forgiveness.

Jesus began His public ministry in Galilee, home territory for Him. On one occasion when He saw the crowds, He went up on the side of a mountain probably near Capernaum, sat down, and began to teach. This teaching is usually called the Sermon on the Mount and is recorded in Matthew 5–7. Luke 6:17–49 also records similar teachings. This lecture was not delivered all at one time, but probably took several days.

Jesus made two references to forgiveness in His teaching about prayer (Matt. 6:5–15). He gave His disciples a Model Prayer, usually called the Lord's Prayer, which teaches us to praise and glorify God first, then to pray about our daily needs and necessities. Jesus' Model Prayer includes this petition related to forgiveness: "Forgive us for doing wrong, as we forgive others" (Matt. 6:12). As in no other place in the prayer, Jesus amplified this particular request: "If you forgive others for the wrongs they do to you, your Father in heaven will forgive you. But if you don't forgive others, your Father will not forgive your sins" (Matt. 6:14–15).

A disciple or Christ follower cannot pray for forgiveness without having a sense of sin and realizing the necessity of asking for forgiveness. The petition in Jesus' Model Prayer is a frightening one and a startling warning about forgiveness. Does it really mean that if we refuse to forgive others, God will refuse to forgive us? Surely not, we think, for God forgives a confessing, repenting, believing sinner. But Jesus presents a principle that strongly binds together forgiveness of others and God's forgiveness of us. Jesus makes it clear that we must forgive if we are to be forgiven.

Jesus' statement about forgiveness relates to His other teachings that the gospel is bound up in our loving God with our whole being and loving others as we love ourselves. Just as these two parts of the greatest commandment cannot be separated, neither can we separate forgiving and being forgiven. We are all sinners in need of God's forgiveness. Jesus is our model. As Christ followers emulating Jesus, we are to be kind, compassionate, and forgiving to others.

Jesus' teaching about forgiveness in the Sermon on the Mount means that we must heal breaches with others, settle arguments and disagreements, and forget the wrong or sin committed against us. It means we are to see the sin no longer and put it behind us. Only then can we expect to receive God's forgiveness. To be forgiven, we must forgive.[2]

Jesus reinforced this teaching a number of other times in His ministry. He concluded His lesson to the disciples about the fig tree, which He had cursed, with these words: "Whenever you stand up to pray, you must forgive what others have done to you. Then your Father in heaven will forgive your sins" (Mark 11:25).

In the Sermon on the Mount, He drew a similar parallel with judging others. "Don't condemn others, and God won't condemn you. God will be as hard on you as you are on others! He will treat you exactly as you treat them" (Matt. 7:1; see also Luke 6:37). "First, take the log out of your own eye. Then you can see how to take the speck out of your friend's eye" (Matt. 7:5). Chapters

9 and 11 examine more closely forgiving others and the relationship of prayer to forgiveness.

Jesus, the Storyteller

Jesus was such an outstanding storyteller and told stories and parables so frequently that some Bible scholars think storytelling was His preferred method of teaching. In His stories, Jesus uses something familiar in life to teach about a concept or principle more difficult to understand.[3] Some of His teachings on forgiveness He conveyed through stories.

Late in His life when He was encountering different reactions to His ministry, Jesus taught His 12 disciples and other followers how to love and forgive. The disciples had argued over who would be the greatest in the kingdom. Jesus used this occasion to teach principles of forgiveness (Matt. 18:21–35). Near the end of the discussion Peter rushed to ask Jesus, "How many times should I forgive someone who does something wrong to me? Is seven times enough?" (Matt. 18:21). He thought he was being quite generous and probably expected to be commended, for in the Bible the number seven means completeness and perfection.

Jesus answered emphatically, "Not just seven times, but seventy-seven times!" (Matt. 18:22). In other words, Jesus believed there should be no limit to forgiveness. Forgiving 77 times means forever. A person should not even keep track of how many times she or he forgives someone else.[4]

Then, to illustrate His point, Jesus told a story of a person forgiven of a great debt. A king called in all his officials and asked them to give an account of what they owed him. One official owed 50 million silver coins and had no money with which to pay the debt. The king ordered the man, his wife, his children, and all his possessions to be sold to pay the debt. The official who owed the money fell on his knees before the king and begged for mercy. "Have pity on me, and I will pay you every cent I owe!" (Matt. 18:26). The king felt sorry for the man, let him go free, and erased the debt.

As the forgiven man was leaving, he encountered someone who owed him 100 silver coins. He grabbed the man by his throat, began choking him, and demanded that he pay the debt. This man, too, got on his knees and begged for mercy, with the same words. "Have pity on me, and I will pay you back" (Matt. 18:29). The response was much different, however. The first man, the one who had been forgiven, refused to have pity and had his debtor imprisoned until he could pay what he owed.

Others heard what had happened and told the story to the king. The king, furious at this action, called the first man back and said: "You're an evil man! When you begged for mercy, I said you did not have to pay back a cent. Don't you think you should show pity to someone else, as I did to you?" (Matt. 18:32–33). The king ordered the man to be tortured until he could pay back his debt.

Failure to pay debts was a serious offense in biblical times. The person who was owed the money could seize the debtor and force him and his family to work until the debt was paid. He could also imprison the debtor and sell his family into slavery to help pay off the debt, hoping that while he was in prison the debtor would sell his possessions. If he could not pay the debt, he might remain in prison forever.[5]

Jesus ended the story with these words: "That is how my Father in heaven will treat you, if you don't forgive each of my followers with all your heart" (Matt. 18:35). The Scriptures give no further interpretation. Jesus left the disciples to draw their own conclusions. But the lesson Jesus taught runs through the New Testament. A person must forgive in order to be forgiven. There is no wrong one person can do to another that can compare with what human beings have done to God. If God forgives us, we must forgive others.

Kingdom Living

Jesus used stories to teach about what it means to live in God's kingdom. Luke 15 includes three stories that are the essence of the good news and God's forgiveness.

On one occasion, tax collectors and sinners had crowded around Jesus to hear Him. The scribes and Pharisees, the religious elite of the day, were incensed that Jesus associated with people they labeled as sinners. They were more concerned about destroying sinners than they were about their salvation. In this setting, Jesus told the stories of the lost sheep (Luke 15:3–7), the lost coin (Luke 15:8–10), and the two sons (Luke 15:11–32).

In biblical times, a shepherd's task was hard and dangerous. Pasture was scarce and terrain rugged. Sheep wandered. The shepherd was responsible for the sheep. Even if he had 100 sheep, a shepherd would leave his flock to search for a single sheep that had strayed away, rejoicing when he found it. Just as there is happiness over finding 1 lost sheep, the heavens rejoice more when one lost sinner turns to God than "over ninety-nine good people who don't need to."[6]

Jesus made the same point in the story of the woman with ten coins who lost one. Palestinian homes in that day were dark and poorly lighted. The earth floors were covered with dried reeds and rushes. It would be extremely hard, almost impossible, to find a lost coin in such a house. But the woman in Jesus' story swept the floor until she found the lost coin. Then she rejoiced. God searches, too, for lost persons, and there is rejoicing in heaven over one person who turns to Him.

Sometimes called the story of the prodigal son, the story of the two sons is actually the story of a loving father. The younger son demanded his inheritance, left home, ran through the money, and wasted his life in riotous living. The older son remained faithful to his father, though he complained at the end of the story when the younger son was forgiven. When the young son came to his senses and returned home, the father welcomed him with open arms, rejoicing that he had been found. More than a story about a son's sins, this parable of Jesus teaches about a father's love—God's love and forgiveness.[7]

At the end of World War II many men like my father were released from military service and returned to their work and families. We moved to Washington, D.C., a burgeoning area. New churches were growing by leaps and bounds, and we became active in one of these thriving churches.

Like any urban center, derelicts, alcoholics, homeless, and depressed people lived on the streets of the downtown area. My father became very involved in a ministry our church had in a downtown mission called Central Union Mission. Often our entire family accompanied him on Saturday nights as he visited and tried to help these men. What an experience this was for me, a fairly new believer.

The thing that stuck in my mind, however, was not the Saturday night ministry at the mission. Instead it is the picture of my father coming into the 8:30 A.M. Sunday worship service at our church the next morning with one or more of these men in tow, much like he had found one lost sheep or coin or son.

Jesus' stories teach us not only about a loving heavenly Father and His joy over one lost and sinful person who comes to Him but also about God's joy in forgiving us.

Lessons from the Things of Life

Occasionally people do not understand a sermon or a story. They have to actually see and experience something rather than just hear about it. This is why ministry projects and activities are so effective in missions education. Jesus sometimes taught by object lessons, though not as often as other ways He used. He wanted to be concrete and clearly symbolize the truth He was trying to teach. Jesus used a real-life object lesson when He forgave a woman caught in sin. John records the experience (John 8).

Jesus had been teaching throughout Galilee and Judea, describing Himself as the Bread of life, the Source of Living Water, and the Light of the world. Some people followed Him. But the Jewish leaders were displeased with Jesus' messages and actions. The people began to take sides.

After a heavy period of teaching, everyone left and Jesus withdrew to the Mount of Olives. The next morning He started teaching again in the temple. Suddenly the Jewish leaders brought in a woman who had been caught in adultery and stood her in the midst of the crowd before Jesus. They accused her of her sin. Then they tried to trick Jesus by using the Law of Moses, which would allow her to be stoned to death. They asked Him what He thought about the situation.

Jesus responded in a strange way. He simply bent over and started writing on the ground with His finger. No one recorded His words. After the Jewish leaders questioned him repeatedly, Jesus stood and said, "If any of you have never sinned, then go ahead and throw the first stone at her!" (John 8:7). Again He bent over and wrote on the ground. The Scriptures say that the people left one by one, beginning with the oldest.

Only Jesus and the accused woman remained at the

scene. The rest of the dialogue is a beautiful and concrete illustration of forgiveness.

"Jesus stood up and asked her, 'Where is everyone? Isn't there anyone left to accuse you?' 'No sir,' the woman answered. Then Jesus told her, 'I am not going to accuse you either. You may go now, but don't sin anymore'" (John 8:10–11).

Adultery was a serious matter in biblical times. The Law of Moses stated that a woman caught in adultery, as well as the man, were to be killed (Lev. 20:10; Deut. 22:22–24). The witnesses were to be the first to throw the stones. The Jewish leaders in this story were correct in their interpretation of the Law. However, it is interesting to note that they only accused the woman and not the man who was also involved in the act of adultery.[8]

In this life experience, Jesus taught the lesson of compassion and forgiveness. Who among them, or us, has never sinned? Was it their role, or is it ours, to judge others? Jesus did not condone what the woman had done nor did He ignore the sin. He told her to leave her life of sin. Jesus is always ready to forgive sin, but true confession and repentance mean a change of heart.

The Unforgivable Sin

Everything within me did not want to deal with Jesus' teaching about the unforgivable or unpardonable sin. First, I am not sure I even begin to understand this teaching of Jesus. We don't seem to talk about this in church as much now as we did in my childhood and teenaged years. And I fear misinterpretation on my part.

As I worked on this book manuscript, I discussed my misgivings about this teaching of Jesus with my brother, a retired longtime pastor whose biblical and theological views I respect greatly. One of his greatest fears, he told me, was that he would actually commit the unpardonable sin through his preaching or ministry. Jesus' teachings about the unforgivable sin are recorded in Luke 12:8–12, Matthew 12:22–32, and Mark 3:28–29.

- *"If you tell others that you belong to me, the Son of Man will tell God's angels that you are my followers. But if you reject me, you will be rejected in front of them. If you speak against the Son of Man, you can be forgiven, but if you speak against the Holy Spirit, you cannot be forgiven"* (Luke 12:8–10).
- *"If you are not on my side, you are against me. If you don't gather in the harvest with me, you scatter it. I tell you that any sinful thing you do or say can be forgiven. Even if you speak against the Son of Man, you can be forgiven. But if you speak against the Holy Spirit, you can never be forgiven, either in this life or in the life to come"* (Matt. 12:30–32).
- *"I promise you that any of the sinful things you say or do can be forgiven, no matter how terrible those things are. But if you speak against the Holy Spirit, you can never be forgiven. The sin will be held against you forever"* (Mark 3:28–29).

Jesus' teaching about the unforgivable sin is included in a broader context that deals with believers confessing Christ before other persons. One writer expresses this as courageous confession. Controversy raged after Jesus healed a blind and mute demon-possessed man. The background for this teaching was the ever-increasing controversy between Jesus and the religious leaders of His day. The Pharisees accused Jesus of being in league with or under the authority of the devil. Rather than seeing God's hand in the work of Jesus, the Pharisees saw Satan's power. In essence they were calling a work of God a work of Satan.

Jesus warned His followers to beware of hypocrisy. They should not pretend to be something they were not or to hide the truth. He also urged His followers not to be afraid when persecuted or criticized, but to trust God Who cared about them.

Finally, Jesus encouraged His followers to speak up for and affirm Him. He made it clear that denial or criticism of Himself can be forgiven as in the case of some of His family members or Peter (see chap. 8). However, when a person is so hardhearted or evil that she or he attributes the work of the Holy Spirit to Satan, or blasphemes the Holy Spirit, that is a sin that will not be forgiven.

This act is deliberately refusing to acknowledge God's power in Christ and willfully turning one's back on God. When a person rejects God or denies the work of the Holy Spirit, that person has no other avenue to God, confession and repentance, or God's forgiveness. In such a state repentance is impossible.[9]

As we read the New Testament, especially Jesus' teachings, we find many other references related to forgiveness. We cannot read the texts about the expectations of the Christian life, God's activity in people's lives, or Jesus' life and teachings without seeing forgiveness expressed.

Questions for Thought and Discussion

1. Why do you think Jesus couched a teaching about forgiveness in the context of prayer?

2. How would you describe the relationship between forgiving and being forgiven, or judging and being judged? What does this have to do with the meaning of the Christian life?

3. What conclusions do you draw from the story of the unforgiving debtor? How does it apply to a Christ follower today?

4. What do you see as the main point in Jesus' stories about the lost sheep, lost coin, and lost son? How does this point reflect your attitude and actions about those who are not Christians?

5. How do you react when others are caught in sin? When others are forgiven? What are some ways you can help such persons?

6. How would you describe Jesus' reply to the Pharisees when they accused Him of serving Satan? How would you define the unforgivable sin in your own words?

7. What other teachings or activities in the New Testament remind you of God's forgiveness? How do you apply them to your life?

---

[1] J. M. Price, *Jesus the Teacher*, rev. ed. (Nashville: Convention Press, 1981), 109–11.
[2] Concepts from Barclay M. Newman and Philip C. Stine, *A Handbook on the Gospel of Matthew* (New York: United Bible Societies, 1989), 171–74; Clifton J. Allen, ed., *The Broadman Bible Commentary* (Nashville: Broadman Press, 1969), 8:116; William Barclay, *The Gospel of Matthew*, rev. ed. (Philadelphia: Westminster Press, 1975), 1:220–25.
[3] Price, *Jesus the Teacher*, 103.
[4] *The Learning Bible*, Contemporary English Version (New York: American Bible Society, 2000), 1779–80.
[5] *Life Application Study Bible*, New International Version (Wheaton, IL: Tyndale House Publishers, Inc., 1991), 1690.
[6] William Barclay, *The Gospel of Luke*, rev. ed. (Philadelphia: Westminster Press, 1975), 206–8.
[7] Ibid., 211–13.
[8] *The Learning Bible*, 1968.
[9] Robert J. Dean, *Layman's Bible Book Commentary* (Nashville: Broadman Press, 1983), 17:81–82; Clair M. Crissey, *Layman's Bible Book Commentary*, 15:69–70; Clifton J. Allen, ed., *The Broadman Bible Commentary* (Nashville: Broadman Press, 1970), 9:106; Clifton J. Allen, ed., *The Broadman Bible Commentary* (Nashville: Broadman Press, 1969), 8:148–49; Barclay, *The Gospel of Luke*, 164–65.

7

How Did Jesus Model Forgiveness?

Jesus took the initiative in forgiveness and showed that no one is beyond forgiveness if the person repents.

Corrie Ten Boom, her sister, and thousands of other women prisoners experienced terrible cruelty and humiliation at Ravensbruck, one of the infamous World War II Nazi concentration camps.

After the war, she lived in Holland but on one occasion returned to defeated Germany where she had the opportunity to speak of God's love and forgiveness. Upon seeing a balding, heavyset man in a gray overcoat, clutching a brown felt hat in his hands, she was overcome with strong emotions. In Ten Boom's mind, she was seeing another man from her past—a blue uniformed guard, a visored cap with skull and crossbones, and a leathered crop swinging from his belt. The man now making his way to the front of the room had been one of the cruelest guards at Ravensbruck. With his hand thrust out toward Ten Boom, he acknowledged his gratefulness for her message of God's forgiveness. While it is doubtful that he

Matthew 9:2–8; 9:4–6; 27:54

Mark 2:6–12; 2:5

Luke 5:17–26; 7:36–50; 7:39; 7:44–47; 7:48; 7:50; 23:34; 23:39; 23:40–41; 23:43

John 4:5–42; 8:3–11

Acts 6:7

James 1:22

remembered Corrie Ten Boom—after all, she was only one of thousands of women prisoners—she remembered him.

For this man, the miracle of all miracles had happened. God had forgiven him for his cruelty during the war. Now he asked Ten Boom also to forgive him. She agonized over her answer. How could she forgive this man? After all, her sister died a slow and terrible death at Ravensbruck. And she could never completely forget her horrific experiences there. Though God had forgiven her for her sins time and time again, Ten Boom found forgiving this man with his outstretched hand one of the hardest things she ever had to do. But the will to forgive won out over her emotions not to forgive. Corrie Ten Boom forgave this former guard who had so abused her. They had indeed become one in Christ.[1]

Jesus not only taught about forgiveness, He practiced it. And He expects His followers to practice it as well. The New Testament writer James reminds us that we are not merely to listen to the Word, but to do what it says (James 1:22). He could also have stated that we should not only teach but also practice what we teach—precisely what Jesus did. He modeled the words of His teachings about forgiveness. He forgave others. He could forgive sinners because He had the divine power and authority to do so, but He also forgave those who wronged Him personally.

This chapter explores some personal examples of Jesus' forgiveness. Though the Bible includes many examples of His acts of forgiveness, we will examine only six: a Samaritan woman, a crippled man, a sinful woman, another sinful woman who anointed Jesus, the criminal on the cross, and Jesus' murderers.

A Samaritan Woman

Only John records the beautiful story of Jesus' encounter with the woman at the well (4:5–42). When the encounter took place, Jesus was traveling from Judea to Galilee early in His ministry to set up His base of operations there.

The trip itself was unusual. The quickest route of travel from Judea to Galilee was through Samaria, which lay between Judea to the south and Samaria to the north. Most Jews in Jesus' day, however, took an alternate route to circumvent Samaria. They crossed the Jordan River in Judea, traveled north on the other side, and crossed the river again below the Sea of Galilee to enter Galilee. Jesus determined not to circumvent, but to go through Samaria.

The Jews of Jesus' day hated the Samaritans, considering them half-breeds and unfaithful to the God of Israel. These deep-seated feelings of hatred and animosity went back years and years to the time Assyria defeated the Northern Kingdom of Israel in 722 B.C. Assyria took most of the people into captivity, but left the poorest people in the region of Samaria. The Assyrians imported foreigners into Samaria, who brought their worship with them. The Samaritan remnant intermarried with the incoming foreigners and ultimately lost their racial purity. In a sense they lost their right to be called Jews.

This was not the result, however, when the Babylonians conquered the Southern Kingdom. Even in captivity those Jews did not lose their identity. Eventually the exiles returned to Jerusalem and began to rebuild the Temple. The Samaritans offered to help their southern neighbors, but were rebuffed by the Jews.

The Samaritans developed their own distinctive religious practices. They later founded a rival temple or alternate worship center to the Temple in Jerusalem, located on Mount Gerizim in the middle of Samaria. Animosity was mutual between the Jews and Samaritans. The Jews considered Samaritans inferior to them and wanted no contact. Thus, they even avoided traveling through Samaria.[2]

In this Bible story Jesus and His disciples entered Samaria rather than going around it. About noon Jesus stopped at a well near the town of Sychar to rest while His disciples went into town to get food. This well, called Jacob's well, was significant in Jewish history and had ties to both Jacob and Joseph in the Old Testament. The well was deep and fed by water that seeped in from rain and dew. One had to have something with which to draw the water from the well.

While Jesus rested, a woman came alone to draw water. Normally women drew water in the morning and evening when it was not so hot, probably also using these occasions to socialize. But this woman came to the well at noon, no doubt to avoid contact with the other women. She was a social outcast, likely considered the lowest-type woman and shunned in town. She had been married five times, but was now living with a man who was not her husband.

Jesus' encounter with this woman was also unusual, but it changed her life. Jesus asked her for a drink of water. She was probably astonished that He talked to her at all. Not only was He a man and she a woman, but He was a Jew and she a Samaritan. Jewish men, especially rabbis or teachers, were forbidden to talk to women in public in that society. And Jews had little to do with Samaritans. Jesus broke through the barriers of nationality and traditions.[3]

Their dialogue followed a pattern. Jesus first picked up on her request for water and her response, identifying Himself as Living Water. In essence He revealed His identity as the Messiah Who could banish thirst forever and give eternal life. The woman took His remark literally, however. She did not understand the spiritual and eternal matters of which He spoke. She understood only physical water and how she would no longer have to come to the well each day to face humiliation.

Jesus then asked the woman to go and bring her husband back with her. Imagine what she was thinking! How could Jesus know the deplorable and immoral life she led? The woman immediately changed the subject to the proper place to worship God. Was it Mount Gerizim, as the Samaritans believed? Or was it the Temple in Jerusalem as the Jews believed? She could not sidetrack Jesus, however. He erased the place of worship as the real issue in their conversation. True worship, according to Jesus, involves an attitude and a spirit. We can find God and worship God anywhere.

Jesus stressed to the woman the unique place of the Jews in God's plan. As the woman alluded to the eventual coming of the Messiah and how He would reveal all this to the people, Jesus identified Himself to her as that Messiah.

The disciples returned with lunch, surprised to find Jesus talking with a Samaritan woman. The woman dropped her water jar, ran back to town, and told everyone of her extraordinary experience with Jesus. She wanted to share her discovery of this amazing person. A changed woman, she was filled with gratitude and thanksgiving. She could leave her past and have a whole new future. In spite of her reputation, the townspeople heard her testimony, for they went out to the well to see Jesus. Many of the Samaritans put their faith in Jesus because of the woman's testimony. They asked Jesus to stay with them so they might know Him better.

Jesus modeled forgiveness in a public place with a hated Samaritan woman who was living openly in sin, and other Samaritans, members of a mixed race. He also revealed the universality of the gospel. Jesus' good news is for every person regardless of race, sex, social position, or past sins.

A Crippled Man

Three Gospel writers, Matthew (9:2–8), Mark (2:6–12), and Luke (5:17–26), report Jesus' healing of the crippled man. Jesus had returned to Galilee to begin His ministry of teaching, preaching, and healing, seemingly freer to do His work in His home area.

During this period Jesus began to experience opposition and rejection as He performed miracles. He healed a government official's son, Peter's mother-in-law, a leper, and many others. The first miracles of healing were somewhat private. But the healing of the leper is apparently the straw that broke the camel's back. The leper, overjoyed with his good fortune, got the word out about his healing and Jesus had to withdraw to desert places to teach. In a sense, His public ministry was momentarily stopped.

When Jesus entered Capernaum, the town where He lived, His healing ministry again took on a more public tone. Four men attempted to bring a crippled man lying on a mat into the house where Jesus was teaching. They must have heard of Jesus' healing miracles and had hope for their friend. The room was noisy and so crowded that there was standing room only. Pharisees and scribes, religious leaders of the day, joined the group, perhaps not with the purest motives. There was no way the men could get their friend into the room and into Jesus' presence.

These ingenious and determined men could not be deterred from their mission, however. They took the crippled man, mat and all, up the stairs to the housetop. They made a hole in the flat roof and lowered the mat into the middle of the room before Jesus. When Jesus saw the faith of the four men, He spoke to the crippled man, "My friend, your sins are forgiven" (Mark 2:5).

"Jesus must think He is God," the observing legalistic scribes thought to themselves. They were always trying to catch Jesus in some violation of the Law. Their theological minds were shocked and they were angry. After all, they believed, only God could forgive sins. Who did Jesus think He was to show no respect for God or God's power? These leaders had a hard choice to make. They could either believe Jesus is divine and has the power to forgive sin, or they could accuse him of blasphemy. They chose the latter.[4] Jesus knew what was in the minds of the scribes.

"Why are you thinking such evil things? Is it easier for me to tell this crippled man that his sins are forgiven or to tell him to get up and walk? But I will show you that the Son of Man has the right to forgive sins here on earth" (Matt. 9:4–6).

Jesus could do both things He asked in His question, that is, forgive sins and heal the man. He is God. Both tasks are equally easy for Him. He has the power and authority to forgive sins. Not only could Jesus remove leprosy as He had done in the healing immediately preceding this one, He could also remove sin and restore a relationship with God. He has the power to heal both physical and spiritual sickness. Jesus' first concern in this case was the man's spiritual condition, but He met both needs. That day Jesus proved He was God and demonstrated His power to forgive sins. He modeled forgiveness.

A Sinful Woman

Chapter 6 briefly examines this story about a sinful woman caught in adultery in light of Jesus' *teachings* on forgiveness. Here, on closer examination, we see it as an *example* of Jesus' forgiveness. John 8:3–11 records the story. Most scholars think this story was not originally in John's Gospel where he placed it. In fact, it was not included in the earliest manuscripts of the New Testament. Most scholars agree, however, that the experience is authentic history and a true story, but probably not a part of this Gospel when John first wrote it.[5]

You will recall that the scribes and Pharisees brought a woman caught in adultery into the temple where Jesus was teaching. After explaining the penalty called for by the Law of Moses, death by stoning, the Pharisees asked Jesus what He thought. Theirs was a trick question. They thought they would have Jesus either way He answered.

Jesus knew that the Jewish penalty for adultery was stoning. But the Jews could not use capital punishment without Roman consent. If Jesus said they should stone the woman, He violated Roman law in pronouncing a death sentence without Roman authority. The scribes and Pharisees were most concerned with condemning the woman. Jesus, however, was concerned with her salvation.

Through this experience Jesus taught the religious leaders a lesson (see chap. 6). The way He responded to their effort to trap Him and His response to the woman show the love, compassion, and mercy that are so much a part of Jesus' relationship with people. In essence, He gave the sinful woman a chance to change her life completely so she could receive forgiveness.

Another Sinful Woman

Only Luke records the account of the sinful woman who anointed Jesus' feet while He ate in the home of a Pharisee (7:36–50). This experience, during Jesus' Galilean ministry, offers a beautiful example of Jesus' compassion toward sinners.

Jesus accepted the invitation of Simon the Pharisee to eat at his home. Just as Jesus sometimes ate with tax collectors and sinners, He also sometimes ate with Pharisees. The Pharisees, which means "the separate ones," were a powerful group within the Jewish community, strict about Jewish laws. They met in private homes to worship, pray, and study the Scriptures.[6] It would not be unusual for Simon to invite Jesus to his home, for Jesus was a rabbi and considered by many a great teacher. Simon might also have wanted to see for himself whether Jesus was really what He said He was. Pharisees believed that only God could forgive sins. Jesus, this so-called teacher, had been claiming this power and authority for Himself.

According to the custom of that day, people ate with their right hand while reclining on their left side on couches with their feet stretched out behind. Wealthy people like Simon usually had homes built around an open courtyard. It was not unusual for people to come in to hear a learned teacher. Jesus was probably in this reclining position when the woman anointed His feet.

When this sinful woman, possibly a prostitute, found out that Jesus was at Simon's house, she bought a bottle of perfume to bring to the house. In addition to the value of the perfume inside, the bottles themselves were expensive, carved from a soft stone called alabaster. The woman came into the house, stood behind Jesus, and began to cry, washing His feet with her tears, then drying them with her hair. She kissed His feet and poured the expensive perfume on them.

Simon was shocked that Jesus let the woman touch Him. He said to himself, "If this man really were a prophet, he would know what kind of woman is touching him! He would know that she is a sinner!" (Luke 7:39). According to Jewish law, someone who touched a sinner was therefore unclean himself and banished from the community.[7]

Jesus responded to Simon as He so often did in His teaching with an object lesson. He told a story in which two people were in debt to a moneylender. Moneychangers set up tables in the courtyard of the Temple where Jews from outside Jerusalem could change their money into the special kind of money used in the Temple.[8] One debtor owed the moneylender 500 silver coins and the other owed 50. However, neither debtor could repay the moneylender. Amazingly the moneylender excused both debts. When asked by Jesus which debtor would be most grateful to the moneylender, Simon gave the obvious answer—the debtor who owed more.

Jesus affirmed Simon's response, then turned to the woman and said to Simon: *"Have you noticed this woman? When I came into your home, you didn't give me any water so I could wash my feet. But she has washed my feet with her tears and dried them with her hair. You didn't greet me with a kiss, but from the time I came in, she has not stopped kissing my feet. You didn't even pour olive oil on my head, but she has poured expensive perfume on my feet. So I tell you that all her sins are forgiven, and that is why she has shown great love. But anyone who has been forgiven for only a little will show only a little love"* (Luke 7:44–47).

Jesus' statement is one of real condemnation of Simon. Good manners prescribed that a host usually placed his hand on the guest's shoulder as he entered the home and gave him a kiss of peace. The host also usually poured cool water over the dusty feet clad in sandals to both clean and make the feet feel comfortable. And, the host usually placed a sweet smelling substance on the guest's head. Simon had done none of these courtesies for Jesus.

Jesus spoke a sharp contrast between Simon's rudeness and the woman's actions. He turned to the woman and said, "Your sins are forgiven" (Luke 7:48). As usual, His authority to forgive sins was questioned. Again Jesus spoke to the woman. "Because of your faith, you are now saved. May God give you peace!" (Luke 7:50).

Perhaps this was not the woman's first encounter with Jesus. She might have heard Him teach or speak earlier and was drawn to Him. There is some thought that Jesus had already forgiven her and in this incident she expresses her gratitude to Him. He refers to her faith, not the love that she seems to be expressing here.[9]

Jesus clearly contrasted the actions and attitudes of the Pharisee with those of the sinful woman. Simon had neglected the common social courtesies: washing Jesus' feet, anointing His head with oil, and offering the kiss of greeting. The woman, however, used her tears, the expensive perfume, and her kisses all on Jesus' feet. It was the grateful sinful woman, not the self-righteous religious leader, whose sins were forgiven.[10] Again, Jesus proved He had the authority and could forgive sins because He is God.

Forgiveness from the Cross

Jesus went to the Cross to take the world's sins upon Him and offer a way of forgiveness. That day He became the atoning, perfect, and final sacrifice for the sins of humanity. It is beyond our ability to understand, however, how He could express specific forgiveness during that horrible experience. Only two such examples are recorded and only by Luke in his Gospel. As He hung on the Cross, Jesus forgave those who put Him to death and He forgave one of the criminals.

The final three days of Jesus' life on earth were days of pain, trauma, agony, torture, rejection, disappointment, denial from His closest companions, and abandonment. Between Thursday night and Saturday of Holy Week, Jesus experienced His arrest, trial, death sentence, crucifixion, and burial.

Jesus was on the Cross six hours that Friday, now called Good Friday, from 9:00 A.M. until 3:00 P.M. As many times as I have read the Old Testament prophecies or the actual account of His crucifixion, I have no real comprehension of the agony Jesus suffered that day for you and for me. The Roman method of crucifixion for criminals was cruel, painful, and brutal beyond description. They whipped Jesus with thongs on which they attached pieces of metal or bone that could rip His flesh to shreds. His accusers and executioners mocked and ridiculed Him cruelly. Nails were driven through His hands and feet and His arms stretched out on the Cross. The soldiers gambled for His clothes at His feet. And, they placed Him on a cross between two other crosses on which hung criminals.

In those early hours on the Cross, Jesus looked at the people responsible for His death and uttered these words: "Father, forgive these people! They don't know what they're doing" (Luke 23:34). Who were these people? They were the Jewish leaders, Roman politicians, and soldiers. But perhaps we were all included in Jesus' reference to "these people," because we are all sinful people. Jesus' prayer is redemptive because His dying was redemptive. He prayed for these people who did not realize what they were doing so that they might experience divine forgiveness.

By dying on the Cross, Jesus opened up the way to salvation for these and all people. Some of the people at the death scene apparently had a change of heart. As Jesus died, the Temple curtain tore in two, the earth shook, graves opened, and rocks split apart. The soldiers and the officer in charge were frightened and said, "This man really was God's Son!" (Matt. 27:54). It was not long before many priests put their faith in Jesus (Acts 6:7).

Jesus was put to death as a common criminal, with actual criminals hanging on crosses on each side of Him.

One criminal insulted Jesus. "Aren't you the Messiah? Save yourself and save us" (Luke 23:39). The other criminal told off the first one. "Don't you fear God? Aren't you getting the same punishment as this man? We got what was coming to us, but he didn't do anything wrong" (Luke 23:40–41). Apparently the second criminal understood that Jesus was innocent.

The second criminal then turned to Jesus and asked to be remembered when Jesus came into power in His kingdom later that day. The criminal saw beyond that awful moment, believed, and had hope and faith. At that moment Jesus said these words to the criminal: "I promise that today you will be with me in paradise" (Luke 23:43). The criminal would go where Jesus was going, forgiven and in paradise.

Questions for Thought and Discussion

1. What did the Samaritan woman do as a result of her encounter with Jesus? How should her response influence your actions? What does Jesus' example with her teach about inclusiveness?

2. Why do you think Jesus forgave the crippled man before He healed him? Has your faith ever led to the forgiveness of someone else? If so, how?

3. What kind of response might you make if someone were brought into your presence personally or into your church, accused of a gross and immoral sin? What did Jesus do? How might His model change your response?

4. What does the example of Jesus forgiving the woman who anointed Him with expensive perfume mean in

today's world? Have you ever acted like Simon, the Pharisee? If so, how? How have you responded to Jesus like the sinful woman did?

5. Explain the meaning of Jesus' forgiveness on the Cross, both His forgiveness of all people and of the criminal beside Him.

[1]David Augsburger, *The New Freedom of Forgiveness,* 3rd ed. (Chicago: Moody Press, 2000), 45–47, citing Corrie Ten Boom, *Tramp for the Lord* (Old Tappan, NJ: Fleming H. Revell, 1974), 55–57, and Corrie Ten Boom, "I'm Still Learning to Forgive," *Guideposts* (Carmel, NY: Guideposts, 1972).
[2]James E. Carter, *Layman's Bible Book Commentary* (Nashville: Broadman Press, 1984), 18:40; William Barclay, *The Gospel of John,* rev. ed. (Philadelphia: Westminster Press, 1975), 1:140–41.
[3]*Life Application Study Bible,* New International Version (Wheaton, IL: Tyndale House Publishers, Inc., 1991), 1879; Barclay, *The Gospel of John,* 1:139, 142.
[4]Johnnie C. Godwin, *Layman's Bible Book Commentary* (Nashville: Broadman Press, 1979), 16:31–32.
[5]Carter, *Layman's Bible Book Commentary,* 18:67.
[6]*The Learning Bible,* Contemporary English Version (New York: American Bible Society, 2000), 1711.
[7]*The Learning Bible,* 1888; William Barclay, *The Gospel of Luke,* rev. ed. (Philadelphia: Westminster Press, 1975), 94–95.
[8]*The Learning Bible,* 1786.
[9]Robert J. Dean, *Layman's Bible Book Commentary* (Nashville: Broadman Press, 1983), 17:57.
[10]*Life Application Study Bible,* 1811.

8

Whom Did God Forgive in the New Testament?

Everyone who repented of sin, confessed it, and trusted God. Peter's life is a model of human sin and forgiveness in the New Testament.

Agnes Gonxha Bojaxhiu, born in Macedonia, joined a religious order when she was 18, took the name Teresa, and was sent immediately to India where she remained for the rest of her life.

In 1948 the church gave Teresa permission to leave her convent as a teacher and work among the poor of Calcutta. That same year she took Indian citizenship and founded a religious order called the Missionaries of Charity which works with the poor not only in Calcutta but also in 50 other cities in India and in 30 other countries. They minister to the needs of hurting and desperate people by providing food and

Matthew 12–13; 4:20; 10:2–4; 15:15; 18:21; 14:28–31

Mark 1:21,29–31; 1:17–18; 3:17; 3:13–19; 8:29; 10:28; 11:21; 8:33; 5:35–43; 9:7; 26:30–46; 14:53,55–56

Luke 5:10; 5:1–11; 6:12–16; 12:14; 24:34

John 1:42–44; 1:35–42; 1:42; 13:38; 13:31–38; 18:12–14,19–23; 18:17; 18:25; 18:27; 20:9; 21:15; 21:15–16; 21:9

Acts 1:13; 2–12; 15; 10–11; 15:13; 22:3; 26:4–8; 18:3; 22:4–5; 7:57 to 8:1; 8:1–3; 9:1–2; 26:9–11; 9:3–19; 22:6–21; 26:13–23; 9:4; 9:15

Galatians 1:13

Philippians 3:5–6; 3:5

1 Peter

2 Peter

operating hospitals, schools, orphanages, youth centers, and shelters for lepers and the dying poor.

Mother Teresa, as this missionary came to be known, received the Nobel Peace Prize in 1979 for her work with the poor. This committed woman devoted her life to ministering to the disadvantaged and marginal people of the world. She spread hope where there seemed to be no hope, demonstrating God's love and forgiveness in a remarkable way.[1]

Because we have experienced God's love and forgiveness, we can in turn show it to others as Christians, following the example of people like Mother Teresa, Peter, and Paul. Often those who have experienced weaknesses and done things they wish they hadn't done also experience God's transforming power and become highly effective in ministry and witness. This was especially true in the lives of Peter and Paul, one of whom denied his Lord and the other who persecuted Christ followers. They are among the best New Testament illustrations of people who received God's forgiveness, though they represented backgrounds, lifestyles, spiritual gifts, special abilities, and modes of ministry that were quite different.

A small-town boy, Peter had little education and was a fisherman by trade. Paul, on the other hand, was a city boy from a good Jewish family, highly educated and trained, a scholar, and committed with passion and zeal to persecuting his Jewish brothers who believed Jesus was the Messiah.

In spite of their differences, these men had at least three things in common. Each had an encounter with Jesus Christ and experienced forgiveness for their sins. Each of their lives was turned around in dramatic ways, causing them to go in a new and completely different direction. And after their inner transformations, each committed themselves fully to furthering the work of God's kingdom.

The Big Fisherman Becomes a Rock

Originally from the town of Bethsaida in Galilee, Peter, whose birth name was Simon, was married and maintained a home in Capernaum (Mark 1:21,29–31). The son of John, he had one brother, Andrew (John 1:42–44). In one of His earliest miracles, Jesus healed Peter's mother-in-law.

Located on the northern shore of Lake Galilee, Capernaum was an important fishing town and was also a Roman outpost where soldiers collected taxes.[2] Jesus moved from Nazareth to Capernaum (Matt. 12–13) and engaged in His early public ministry in that region. Peter was a fisherman in partnership with James and John, sons of Zebedee (Luke 5:10).

John the Baptist, Jesus' cousin and forerunner, preached in this area and called people to repentance, influencing Andrew, Peter's brother, so much so that Andrew sought out Jesus. Andrew immediately took Simon Peter to Jesus, Whom Andrew identified as the Messiah (John 1:35–42). When Jesus saw Simon, He changed his name: "Simon, son of John, you will be called Cephas" (John 1:42). The name *Cephas* could be translated as *Peter*; both names meant "rock." From that point on, Peter began to follow Jesus and his life took on a rocklike quality.

Peter's call was simple, yet dramatic. While Jesus was walking along the shore of the lake, He saw Peter and Andrew fishing. Jesus called them, along with James and John, to bring in people rather than fish. Their response to Jesus' call was incredible. The four men dropped their nets and went with Jesus *right then,* or *immediately* (Matt. 4:20; Mark 1:17–18; Luke 5:1–11). They left everything—their occupations, families, and homes—to follow Jesus and become His disciples.

Peter was not the leader of the group; Jesus was. But Peter was the recognized or natural leader of the disciples. He was in the inner circle of three—James, John, and Peter—who were especially close to Jesus (Mark 3:17). Peter's name is placed first in all four listings of the disciples (Matt. 10:2–4; Mark 3:13–19; Luke 6:12–16; Acts 1:13).

Peter no doubt became the spokesman for the group because he was so brash and impulsive. He always seemed to be the first to speak out and speak up. On one occasion Jesus asked the disciples what the people were saying about Him, then what the disciples themselves were saying. Peter jumped in with the response, "You are the Messiah!" (Mark 8:29), indicating his strong faith in Jesus. After Jesus' encounter with the rich man and His teaching about the difficulty of getting into the kingdom, the disciples were amazed and questioned how anyone could ever be saved. Peter reminded the Lord, "Remember, we left everything to be your followers!" (Mark 10:28).

On another occasion Jesus put a curse on a fruitless fig tree in the presence of the disciples. When they came by the withered tree the next morning, it was Peter who first noticed and spoke out: "Teacher, look! The tree you put a curse on has dried up" (Mark 11:21). When Jesus taught about what makes people unclean, that is, what comes out of a person's mouth rather than what goes in, the disciples were afraid that the Pharisees would feel insulted. Jesus tried to explain further, but Peter questioned Him as usual, "What did you mean when you talked about the things that make people unclean?" (Matt. 15:15).

It was Peter who asked Jesus how many times he should forgive someone who wronged him. "Is seven times enough?" (Matt. 18:21). It was Peter who raised the question when Jesus taught about faithful and unfaithful servants. "Did you say this just for us or for everyone?" (Luke 12:41).

Jesus sometimes singled out Peter for teachings intended for the entire group. After Peter had given his magnificent declaration of faith that Jesus was the Messiah, Jesus began to tell His disciples about what would happen to Him. He would suffer terribly, be rejected and killed, and rise to life three days later. He explained clearly what He meant. Peter took Jesus aside and told Him to stop talking like that. "But when Jesus turned and saw the disciples, he corrected Peter. He said to him, 'Satan, get away from me! You are thinking like everyone else and not like God'" (Mark 8:33).

Peter, as one of Jesus' inner circle, was privy to some intimate and special moments with Jesus. Jesus permitted only Peter, James, and John to go with Him to Jairus's home when Jairus's daughter died. Peter saw Jesus raise the little girl from death to life (Mark 5:35–43).

One day Jesus took the inner circle with Him up a high mountain where they could be alone in an experience we call the Transfiguration. Jesus was completely changed in front of these disciples. Impulsive Peter wanted to build three tabernacles, one for Jesus, one for Moses, and one for Elijah. Though Peter did not know what he was talking about, it is commendable that he had such strong faith that he wanted to worship God. The disciples were frightened because they did not understand what was happening. Peter and the two other disciples witnessed a divine experience when God put His blessing on His Son. "The shadow of a cloud passed over and covered them. From the cloud a voice said, 'This is my Son, and I love him. Listen to what he says!'" (Mark 9:7).

All of the disciples went with Jesus to the Mount of Olives after the Passover meal and the Lord's Supper in the upper room. These experiences were during Jesus' last week on earth. Jesus took them into the garden of Gethsemane so He could pray for what lay ahead for

Him. He then took Peter, James, and John further into the garden where He agonized in prayer to the Father. Probably exhausted from all they had experienced in recent and trying days, the inner circle went to sleep while Jesus wrestled over His coming arrest, trial, and execution (Matt. 26:30–46).

The inner circle was with Jesus in the garden when He was arrested. The impetuous Peter pulled out a sword, struck the high priest's servant, and cut off his right ear (John 18:10).

The Rock Crumbles

Though Peter's faith was often great, at times it was also quite weak. Can you identify with him? Perhaps the most graphic example of Peter's weak faith is when he tried to walk on water. Jesus had fed the 5,000, a miracle the disciples witnessed. He instructed the disciples to get into the boat and head home across the lake while He stayed to send the crowd away and to go up on the mountain. Jesus wanted to be alone and pray.

The disciples encountered a fierce storm on the lake, which they battled most of the night. Imagine their exhaustion and terror, enough to set them screaming, when they saw what they thought was a ghost walking toward them on the water. Only Jesus' reassurance that it was He could calm their fears. Brash, impulsive Peter reacted.

"'Lord, if it is really you, tell me to come to you on the water.' 'Come on!' Jesus said. Peter then got out of the boat and started walking on the water toward him. But when Peter saw how strong the wind was, he was afraid and started sinking. 'Save me, Lord!' he shouted. Right away, Jesus reached out his hand. He helped Peter up and said, 'You surely don't have much faith. Why do you doubt?'" (Matt. 14:28–31).

Peter did fine as long as he kept his eyes on Jesus. Only

when he took his eyes off Jesus and focused instead on the storm did he start to sink.

The sin for which we so often remember him is Peter's denial of Jesus during the trials. After the Passover meal and departure of Judas, Jesus warned His disciples, Peter in particular, against desertion (John 13:31–38). Peter affirmed his loyalty by declaring he would die for Jesus. However, Jesus asked Peter: "Would you really die for me? . . . I tell you for certain that before a rooster crows, you will say three times that you don't even know me" (John 13:38).

The disciples kept a low profile while Jesus went through His trials, no doubt fearing for their own safety and in a state of shock and complete insecurity. Annas, the former high priest and Caiaphas's father-in-law, examined Jesus first (John 18:12–14,19–23). Then Jesus was tried and condemned by Caiaphas, the current high priest, and the Jewish council called the Sanhedrin (Mark 14:53,55–65).

Peter and John stayed in close proximity, but just far enough away to avoid danger. They followed Jesus. John followed Him all the way into the courtyard while Peter stayed outside near the gate. John came out and spoke to the servant girl about Peter coming in. As the girl let Peter in, she asked him if he was one of Jesus' followers. Peter replied, "No, I am not!" (John 18:17): denial number one.

It was a cold night in more ways than one. The servants and temple police made a charcoal fire to take off the chill, and Peter joined them as they were warming themselves. One in the group asked Peter if he was one of Jesus' followers. Again Peter denied it. "No, I am not!" (John 18:25): denial number two.

A high priest's servant, a relative of the man whose ear Peter cut off in the garden, asked Peter whether he had seen him in the garden with Jesus. Once more, Peter denied his presence with Jesus (John 18:27): denial number three. Even while Peter was speaking a rooster crowed, bringing to life Jesus' earlier prediction of the three denials. Jesus turned and looked at Peter. Peter remembered the Lord's words and went out and wept bitterly.

Forgiveness: The Crumbled Rock Transformed

Peter must have been not only grief-stricken but also devastated as Jesus died on the Cross, his hopes for the future dashed as his leader died. He lived with the constant memory of his recent denials of his master.

Sunday finally came after that grim Friday and the grief of Saturday. When Mary Magdalene discovered the empty tomb early that morning, she ran quickly to Peter and John with the news. The disciples ran to the tomb to see for themselves. They did not really understand this miracle was going to happen (John 20:9) even though Jesus had told them it would. What a miracle! Jesus did not remain in the grave, but God raised Him from the dead on the third day.

Jesus appeared a number of times to various individuals and groups after His death and before He ascended into heaven, at some point appearing to Peter. When the two disciples who had seen Jesus on the road to Emmaus found the apostles, "they learned from the group that the Lord was really alive and had appeared to Peter" (Luke 24:34). We can only speculate about the conversation during that visit.

The disciples did what most of us do during in a time of grief. They returned to their daily routine and work, trying to forget a bitter experience. The disciples went fishing, but caught nothing after a night's work. The next morning Jesus appeared, though they did not recognize

Him, and told them to fish again. This time they caught so many fish that they could not even drag the net up to the boat. While the disciples were fishing Jesus prepared breakfast for them—bread and cooked fish.

When Peter heard Jesus' voice and realized Who was really on the shore, he reacted in his impulsive way. He was so excited, he put back on the clothes he had taken off while fishing, jumped into the water, and swam to shore. He then returned to help bring in the catch.

Jesus' encounter with Peter on the shore indicates not only that had He forgiven Peter but also that had He work for Peter to do in the kingdom. He asked Peter whether he loved Him more than the others did (John 21:15), referring to love in its highest form. Peter, however, misunderstood and responded to Jesus with a companionship-type love. "Then feed my lambs" (John 21:15), Jesus told him. Jesus asked Peter a second time if he loved Him and Peter responded again that he did. "Then take care of my sheep" (John 21:15–16), Jesus replied. Then Jesus asked a third time.

Peter was hurt because Jesus asked him three times whether he loved his Lord, the same number of times as Peter's denials of Jesus. Again Peter told Jesus of his love for Him, and again Jesus told Peter to feed His sheep. Jesus ended this dialogue with the words, "Follow me" (John 21:19), words identical to those Jesus used when He called Peter the first time. Jesus did indeed have work for Peter to do.

What happened to Peter? Did he follow through on Jesus' instructions? Yes, indeed! Influential in establishing the church in Jerusalem (see the early chapters of Acts), Peter was out on the cutting edge, feeding the sheep and spreading the good news (Acts 2–12; 15). Bold and brash, he continued to speak up for his Lord and was active in the beginning stages of the mission to the Gentiles. God showed Peter in a vision that the good news is not just for the Jews, but also for the Gentiles (Acts 10–11).

Peter served as a bridge in the early church in Jerusalem, where James, the brother of Jesus, was the leader (Acts 15:13). It was Peter who helped hold together the diverse strands of the early Christian movement. While it was Paul, not Peter, who became the apostle to the Gentiles, Peter had the vision that helped Jewish Christians understand that the gospel is for all people. Peter's influence continues through his New Testament writings, 1 and 2 Peter, originally penned to encourage Christians who suffered persecution from the Romans, warn them about false teachers, and exhort them to grow in their faith and knowledge of Jesus.

A Zealous Teacher

Paul's background was as different from Peter's as night is from day. Born into a Jewish family that practiced their faith, Paul was circumcised on the eighth day (Phil. 3:5) and given the Jewish name Saul. He was named after King Saul because they were both from the tribe of Benjamin. Because he was born in Tarsus, a Roman city, he claimed Roman citizenship (Acts 22:3) and carried the Roman name Paul. Tarsus was a bustling city, self-governing, and loyal to Rome.

As a young boy in a Jewish family, Paul was trained in Jewish Scriptures and tradition beginning at home (Acts 26:4–8; Phil 3:5–6) and was enrolled in a synagogue day school at an early age. There he learned the ancient Hebrew language and learned to read and write by copying Scriptures. The family probably spoke Aramaic at home, and because Paul related to the larger community, he also learned Greek. Along the way Paul learned the trade of making tents, which he later used as a means of support (Acts 18:3).

Probably in his teenaged years Paul was privileged to study under Gamaliel, a famous rabbi and member of the Jewish council in Jerusalem who was considered the best teacher of that day (Acts. 22:3). Paul became zealous for the traditions and teachings of his people, becoming a Pharisee and strictly obeying the laws (Phil 3:5).[3]

Paul's strict commitment to Jewish traditions, teachings, and laws probably led to his persecution of fellow Jews who believed Jesus was the Messiah. He was proud that he had made trouble for the Christian church (Acts 22:4–5; Phil. 3:5–6). He watched over the coats of the men who stoned Stephen to death, an action he approved (Acts 7:57 to 8:1).

Paul's great sin was his persecution of the early church. Going from house to house, arresting and jailing men and women (Acts 8:1–3), he threatened followers of the Lord and sought letters from the high priest to arrest even more (Acts 9:1–2). He voted for Christians to be killed and often had them punished (Acts 26:9–11). In essence, he tried to destroy the Christian church (Gal. 1:13). But Paul was a learned man. In order to carry out his mission of persecution, he no doubt knew as much as possible about Jesus and the church, as well as the message of Christianity.

A Dramatic and Transformational Encounter

Luke recounts Paul's conversion experience in Acts 9:3–19, 22:6–21, and 26:13–23. Paul was traveling to Damascus, the capital of Syria, carrying official letters from Jewish leaders that would lead to the arrest of Jews who had accepted Jesus as the Messiah. Normally a journey from Jerusalem to Damascus would take about a week as one traveled via donkeys or mules.

Paul was close to Damascus when suddenly a startling

light flashed around him, a light so bright that he was blinded and fell to the ground. "Saul, Saul, why are you so cruel to me?" he heard a voice asking (Acts 9:4). Paul had no clue who was addressing him until Jesus identified Himself as the one Paul was persecuting. Immediately Paul asked Jesus what He wanted him to do. Jesus told Paul to go into the city and wait for further instructions. Someone who had seen the light but not heard the voice led the blinded Paul into the city.

Ananias, a follower of the Lord, delivered God's message to Paul and restored his sight. God told Paul through Ananias that he "would tell foreigners, kings, and the people of Israel about me" (Acts 9:15). He was to preach the good news to Jews and Gentiles alike. Paul, now a believer in the One he had persecuted, was baptized and moved on with his life of service for his new Lord.

A Complete and Radical Change

Paul's conversion resulted in a complete and radical change in his life. Once controlled by his passionate allegiance to Jewish traditions and teachings, his zeal to following Jesus now guided him. Paul spent the rest of his life trying to fulfill his calling and mission, to tell the good news to the Gentiles.

Space does not permit a detailed description of all that Paul did and experienced for his Lord. The Book of Acts and all of Paul's letters only begin to plumb the depths of his commitment. But we know that he traveled throughout the Roman world on three missionary journeys taking the gospel message, bearing many trials and tribulations, and starting and strengthening churches. And the great theological treatises in Paul's letters, written mostly while he was in prison, continue to educate and inspire.

The lives of Peter and Paul provide vivid, dramatic examples not just of people's sin but also of God's forgiveness and restoration. When God forgives us, He also refreshes and retools us and uses us in His service.

Questions for Thought and Discussion

1. Review your life and background. Include your experience of forgiveness and becoming a Christian as well as your call to service. How does your background equip you for ministry? In what ways have your personal failures affected your service to God?

2. Describe at what times your faith has been strong. What times has your faith been weak? Has there ever been a time when you denied your Lord? If so, revisit that experience in your mind and the forgiveness that followed.

3. What happens when you take your eyes off Jesus and focus instead on the storms of life? What experiences have you had where this happened to you?

4. What does Jesus' instruction to Peter on the beach ("Follow me"; "Feed my sheep") mean to you and other Christ followers today? How do you carry out this instruction?

5. Describe the radical transformation in Paul's life when he met Jesus. Now describe your own conversion experience. How did Paul fulfill the mission God called him to do? What is your mission and how are you fulfilling it?

[1]Robin Chew, "Mother Teresa: Humanitarian" [article online]; www.lucidcafe.com/lucidcafe/library/95aug/motherteresa.html.
[2]*The Learning Bible*, Contemporary English Version (New York: American Bible Society, 2000), 1742.
[3]Trent C. Butler, ed., *Holman Bible Dictionary* (Nashville: Holman Bible Publishers, 1991), 1077–85.

9

What Is Involved When We Forgive Others?

The forgiven have a God-given mandate to forgive others. Forgiving others is the bridge we must pass over to receive forgiveness ourselves.

One of the most difficult things a person must do is forgive another person. Our natural human inclination is to blame others, harbor grudges, nurture anger, and be resentful. We can trace our attitude back to the beginnings of humanity with Adam and Eve and their descendants, especially in the story of Cain and Abel (Gen. 4). Jealousy, anger, and blame led Cain, the first son of Adam and Eve, to murder his younger brother, Abel. You remember the story. Cain was a farmer and Abel a shepherd. Each gave an offering to

Genesis 4; 4:7; 45:4–5; 47–50

Hosea 2:4–5; 3:1; 3:2–5; 2:19–20

Matthew 6:14–15; 7:12; 6:12; 18:22–35; 5:38–39; 6:9–15; 18:21–22; 18:35

Mark 11:25–26; 2:5

Luke 15:32

John 8:7

Acts 12:12; 13:13; 15:37–40

Romans 12:17–21

Ephesians 4:31–32; 4:32

Colossians 3:12–14; 4:10; 3:13

2 Timothy 4:11

Philemon

God, Cain part of his harvest and Abel his firstborn lamb.

The Lord was pleased with Abel and his offering, but not with Cain and his offering. The Bible does not say why God rejected Cain's sacrifice. Perhaps Cain did not offer the best of his harvest or he had an improper attitude. Nevertheless, Cain was so angry that he could not hide his feelings. God warned him, "But you did the wrong thing, and now sin is waiting to attack you like a lion. Sin wants to destroy, but don't let it!" (Gen. 4:7). Cain fell prey to sin, however, rather than doing what was right. He invited Abel to go for a walk with him and while they were out in a field, Cain murdered his brother. God punished Cain severely for this sin.

Forgiveness has both divine and human dimensions. Chapters 1–8 of this book deal primarily with the divine dimension. But what does forgiveness mean from a human perspective? Just as God shows grace and mercy in forgiving us, our forgiveness of others involves acts and attitudes of grace and mercy toward those who have wronged us, which restore relationships and fellowship. Forgiveness pardons or excuses wrongs or cancels debts. It gives up a claim for revenge or resentment and mends a broken relationship. Forgiveness reestablishes trust and forges a new beginning in attitudes and actions.

David Augsburger defines forgiveness this way: "Forgiving is risking a return to conversation and a resumption of relationship. Forgiveness in the New Testament sense is more synonymous with our understanding of reconciliation than with love. The two Greek words for forgiveness are translated most clearly as 'to release or set free' and 'to offer a gift of grace.'"[1] Augsburger further describes forgiveness as a journey or a process and not a quick fix. Forgiveness is a costly task taking time and effort, and follows the example of Christ.

It's Your Fault, Not Mine

Many Christ followers struggle with blame, which affects their ability to forgive others. Blame is finding fault with someone else or holding someone else responsible. A person may blame her parents, spouse, or children. She or he may blame a co-worker or boss, the government, time or lack of time, society as a whole, or even the church.

Our human and sinful nature causes us to minimize our own sins and magnify the blame of others. We are prone to look out for ourselves. After all, if we are always right, we will treat ourselves with mercy and grace, but demand that the other person be punished.

We learn this attitude and acquire this ability innately as small children. According to my mother, my brother, 4 years older, was a master at blaming me. Mother often told us stories of watching from the kitchen window as her toddler daughter and 5-year-old son played in the sandbox. She watched my brother repeatedly dump bucketful after bucketful of sand on top of and in my tight ringlet curls. I always reached the point, she said, when I had had enough and retaliated vehemently with all of my strength. This action always resulted in a 5-year-old yell: "Mom, Bobbie is hitting me. She made me do it." I am not casting stones at my brother for I soon learned to blame others, too.

Mature blame is a much more serious matter, however. Maybe a husband or wife blames the other for a bitter divorce. Perhaps an employee blames a supervisor for her dismissal from work or the downgrading of her responsibilities. Maybe a disgruntled Christian blames a poor Sunday School teacher or weak pastor for his refusal to participate in worship services or other church activities. Maybe a murderer on death row blames his partners in crime or even the victim for his present state. Perhaps a minister blames the pressure and stress of life for his sexual abuse of his own daughters. Maybe a spouse blames the other partner or children for the abuse he or she heaps on them. Or, a teenager blames her parents for lack of attention, which led her to drugs and promiscuity.

Why Should I Forgive You?

Why should we forgive others when it is so difficult? God's love and forgiveness for us should be the motive for forgiveness by a Christ follower. God provided a way of salvation for humanity through His Son, Jesus Christ. Christians must and should want to forgive those who have wronged them because of God's forgiveness. Those who have been forgiven are obligated to forgive. A forgiving spirit ought to characterize Christians. Jesus taught us to forgive and modeled forgiveness with His own life. (See chaps. 6 and 7.)

In several of his letters to the churches, Paul gives instructions for the new life in Christ. He wrote these words to the church at Ephesus.

"Stop being bitter and angry and mad at others. Don't yell at one another or curse each other or ever be rude. Instead, be kind and merciful, and <u>forgive others</u>, just as God forgave you because of Christ" (Eph. 4:31–32, author's emphasis).

Paul reiterates to the church at Colossae that the new life should affect the way they live together as God's people.

"God loves you and has chosen you as his own special people. So be gentle, kind, humble, meek, and patient. Put up with each other and <u>forgive anyone who does you wrong</u>, just as Christ has forgiven you. Love is more important than anything else. It is what ties everything completely together" (Col. 3:12–14, author's emphasis).

Paul also described for the Roman Christians how the followers of Christ should live. Understanding God's forgiveness should make His people more willing to forgive persons who mistreat them. It is a matter of attitudes and actions.

"Don't mistreat someone who has mistreated you. But try to earn the respect of others, and do your best to live at peace with everyone. Dear friends, don't try to get even. Let God take revenge. In the Scriptures the Lord says, 'I am the one to take revenge and pay them back.' The Scriptures also say, 'If your enemies are hungry, give them something to eat. And if they are thirsty, give them something to drink. This will be the same as piling burning coals on their heads.' Don't let evil defeat you, but defeat evil with good" (Rom. 12:17–21).

Forgiveness and love are the motivators for Christ followers to forgive others. The forgiveness of the Old Testament prophet Hosea for his unfaithful wife illustrates this motivation beautifully. Though this Old Testament book is difficult to understand, the marriage theme runs throughout the book. Scholars take different views of Hosea's prophecy. Some think that the marriage is an allegory of God's relationship with Israel. Others think that Hosea presents his marriage experiences as he remembers them later. And, still others believe that Hosea married a temple prostitute as he was told to do.[2]

Hosea was a prophet to the Northern Kingdom of Israel during its ending days of prosperity. The kingdom was declining morally, especially in its oppression of the poor. Hosea prophesied until shortly after the fall of Samaria to Assyria in 722 B.C. The Old Testament prophets Amos, Isaiah, and Micah were his contemporaries. God commanded Hosea, whose name means salvation, to marry a woman who would be unfaithful to him and cause him much grief. Hosea did as God told him and married Gomer, who may have been a temple prostitute in the cult of Baal, the Canaanite fertility god.[3]

Gomer bore three children and each was given a name

signifying a divine message (Hos. 1). Hosea was probably not the father (Hos. 2:4–5). Then, Gomer left Hosea for other men, shattering her marriage. But God spoke to Hosea again. "Go, show your love to your wife again, though she is loved by another and is an adulteress. Love her as the Lord loves the Israelites, though they turn to other gods and love the sacred raisin cakes" (Hos. 3:1 NIV).

Hosea brought Gomer back and loved her (Hos. 3:2–5). He wanted Gomer to repent and receive forgiveness and restoration. Perhaps Hosea's message to her was like God's message to Israel. "I will accept you as my wife forever, and instead of a bride price I will give you justice, fairness, love, kindness and faithfulness. Then you will truly know who I am" (Hos. 2:19–20).

Hosea's experience with Gomer reflects God's experience with Israel. Hosea found Gomer, redeemed her, and brought her home again, fully reconciled. God also seeks us and redeems and reconciles us through His forgiveness of our sins. Both divine and human compassion lead to forgiveness.

We Reap What We Sow

Serious side effects follow when we refuse to forgive another person who has wronged or is perceived to have wronged us. Though I am not a psychologist, I know about many of these effects because I have experienced them personally or observed them in those close to me. If we had it in our power to avoid these effects, we obviously would. Only the power of the Holy Spirit, however, can transform a believer to want to forgive others and to act on that desire.

An unforgiving spirit can result in physical, mental, and emotional stress. You, like me, have probably experienced

symptoms such as these:
- Sleeplessness
- Inability to concentrate
- Bitter tears
- Anger and hurt feelings
- Feelings of helplessness
- Desire to retreat or flee
- Poor work habits
- Tardiness
- Avoidance of responsibilities
- Shortness of breath
- Paralyzed spirit
- Poor eating habits
- Depression
- Apathy
- Propensity for errors
- Lethargy

Hatred and anger are extremely destructive in all of these areas of life. You no doubt could add items to this list. However, it is certain that a bitter and unforgiving spirit takes its toll on the body, mind, and soul.

The spiritual stress caused by unwillingness to forgive is even worse than the physical, mental, or emotional stress. A condemning, revengeful, unforgiving spirit seems to consume a person. Bitterness paralyzes the desire or even the ability to reach God at a time the person needs Him most. The cycle of blame and pain is never-ending unless forgiveness takes place. The cycle just goes on and on with the potential ultimately to destroy.

When we fail to forgive another, we often find it harder or even impossible to worship God, pray, read the Bible, engage in ministry or service, or relate to others. We experience alienation, lack of fellowship, and a broken relationship with God even as these things are true with the offending family member, fellow believer, friend, or enemy.

The worst result of not forgiving others is the effect it has on God's willingness to forgive us. God will not forgive those who do not forgive others. Jesus made this clear in His teachings.

- *"If you forgive others for the wrongs they do to you, your Father in heaven will forgive you. But if you don't forgive others, your Father will not forgive your sins"* (Matt. 6:14–15).

- *"Whenever you stand up to pray, you must forgive what others have done to you. Then your Father in heaven will forgive your sins" (Mark 11:25–26).*

Jesus emphasizes the importance of praying for our own forgiveness. But if we refuse to forgive others, God will refuse to forgive us. We cannot ask for ourselves what we deny to others. Only God's power can enable us to forgive others as God forgives us.

It stands to reason. A bitter and unforgiving heart erects a barrier between that person and the God of love. Each believer has a desire to be right with God and can ask God to remove their bitter, unforgiving spirit. Only then can that person forgive another and experience forgiveness herself.

Feeling Good Again

Forgiveness brings positive results to both the individual who offers forgiveness and to the one who receives it. The one offering forgiveness feels good and whole when she or he follows biblical principles of forgiving others. It is positive, right, and joyful to be kind, merciful, and forgiving (Eph. 4:32). Forgiving others is healthy, wholesome, virtuous, and liberating. It unleashes joy, brings peace, and sets all the best and highest of love in motion. Forgiveness shows grace and mercy and proves obedience. And, the forgiver receives the blessing of revitalized fellowship with another person. Married couples as well as good friends or family members experience this joy after a disagreement followed by forgiveness. Rejoicing and happiness come both to the forgiver and the forgiven.

The person who receives forgiveness rejoices in reconciliation and restored fellowship. In the story sometimes called the parable of the prodigal son, the older brother is jealous and upset because his father lavishes love and pours out forgiveness on his younger brother. After all, the younger brother had demanded his inheritance, then squandered it in riotous living. The father expresses well the sense of joy in forgiveness as he speaks to his oldest son. "My son, you are always with me, and everything I have is yours. But we should be glad and celebrate! Your brother was dead, but he is now alive. He was lost and has now been found" (Luke 15:32).

The Bible includes some wonderful examples of the joys of forgiving others. Joseph, the son of the patriarch Jacob, forgave his brothers for selling him into Egyptian slavery when he was only 17 years old. The brothers had deceived their father by intimating that a wild animal had killed Joseph. Joseph's brothers hated him for being his father's favorite and for his arrogant ways. Joseph, however, had personal integrity and eventually rose to a powerful position as a ruler in the king's government, preparing Egypt to survive a famine by wisely collecting and storing grain.

Sure enough, the famine came, not just in Egypt but in all the neighboring countries as well. Jacob sent his remaining sons to Egypt to buy grain. They had no idea Joseph was still alive, let alone a powerful government official there. It had been 20 years or so since the brothers had last seen him and they did not recognize him. He recognized them, however.

The story is rather involved as to how Joseph tests his brothers. Finally, when the brothers arrived in Egypt the second time, Joseph could no longer contain nor control his feelings. He revealed himself to them with tears of joy. "Yes, I am your brother Joseph, the one you sold into Egypt. Don't worry or blame yourselves for what you did. God is the one who sent me ahead of you to save lives" (Gen. 45:4–5). Not only did Joseph forgive his brothers, but he also moved his father, Jacob, and the entire family to Egypt where he could take care of them during the famine (Gen. 47–50).

Though we have no details of the story, the Apostle Paul apparently forgave the young John Mark. John Mark was Barnabas's cousin (Col. 4:10). His mother, Mary, often opened her home to the apostles (Acts 12:12). John Mark joined Paul and Barnabas on their first missionary journey. For unknown reasons, John Mark left them in the middle of the trip (Acts 13:13).

As they prepared to embark on their second missionary journey, Paul and Barnabas disagreed sharply over whether to take John Mark with them. Paul did not want to take him because John Mark had left them before, abandoning the mission. Paul and Barnabas separated and formed two teams. Paul took Silas with him, and Barnabas took John Mark (Acts 15:37–40).

John Mark was by no means a failure, however, later writing the Gospel of Mark. He later became vital to Paul's ministry (Col. 4:10). Paul commended John Mark as a help to him in the growth of the early church. He asked Timothy to bring John Mark to him in prison (2 Tim. 4:11).

In another of Paul's letters, he pleaded with Philemon to forgive another person. Again, we do not know how the story turned out. Philemon was a wealthy man who probably lived in Colossae and was a member of the church there, using his home for church meetings. Philemon owned slaves as did many during those days. Onesimus, one of Philemon's slaves, ran away to Rome where he met Paul and became a follower of Christ. Paul wrote to Philemon that he was sending Onesimus back to him not just as a slave, but as a brother in Christ. He asked Philemon to accept and forgive Onesimus (Philemon).[4]

Principles of Forgiveness

Many biblical principles of forgiveness have emerged thus far:

- Forgive rather than judge others or cast stones at them (John 8:7).
- Do not resent God's forgiveness of others (Luke 15:32).
- Treat others like you want them to treat you (Matt. 7:12).
- God will forgive us as we forgive others (Matt. 6:12).
- Forgiveness of others opens us to receive forgiveness ourselves (Mark 2:5).
- Forgiveness requires kindness and mercy (Eph. 4:32).
- Forgive as Jesus did (Col. 3:13; Matt. 18:22–35).
- Show patience when suffering wrongs inflicted by others (Matt. 5:38–39).
- Begin the journey of forgiveness with prayer (Matt. 6:9–15).
- Forgiveness is limitless (Matt. 18:21–22).
- Forgiveness must come from the heart (Matt. 18:35).

Questions for Thought and Discussion

1. Do you find it hard to forgive others? Why? How do you do it?

2. How might the story of Cain and Abel have been different if Cain had followed God and forgiveness prevailed? Have you ever gotten so jealous, angry, or full of blame that you wanted to "murder" someone? How did this attitude make you feel? How did it affect your actions?

3. What motivates you to forgive someone who has wronged you? Give an example in your own life.

4. What does Hosea's forgiveness of Gomer teach today's Christ followers about forgiveness?

5. How does an unforgiving spirit affect you physically, mentally, emotionally, and spiritually?

6. How does forgiving another person who has wronged you make you feel? How does it make them react?

7. What is the overall message of the story of Joseph's forgiveness of his brothers? Paul's forgiveness of John Mark? The potential forgiveness by Philemon of Onesimus?

8. Make your own list of principles of forgiveness. How do they relate to you? How do you apply them?

---

[1] David Augsburger, *The New Freedom of Forgiveness*, 3rd ed. (Chicago: Moody Press, 2000), 29.
[2] Billy K. Smith, *Layman's Bible Book Commentary* (Nashville: Broadman Press, 1982), 13:13.
[3] *The Learning Bible*, Contemporary English Version (New York: American Bible Society, 2000), 1583.
[4] *Life Application Study Bible,* New International Version (Wheaton, IL: Tyndale House Publishers, Inc., 1991), 2213.

10

Why Is It Important to Forgive Ourselves?

Because God has forgiven us, and self-forgiveness is essential to live the forgiven life God designed for us.

A couple of years ago it was my privilege to participate in a weeklong wellness retreat, one of the most intense experiences of my life. Most of the participants and their spouses were experiencing forced terminations from their places of ministry and service. I was there seeking healing from a number of losses and bitter feelings about self and others, not the least of which was the death of my husband.

The fruits of forgiving self were most clear to me as I watched the changes in one young woman's life during that week. Because I shared a suite with her and we spent many hours talking, I could almost watch the transformation unfold. Her whole demeanor, outward appearance, facial expression, per-

Genesis 1:26

Psalms 32; 8:5–8; 139: 139:13–14; 139:16b; 51:3–6; 38:3–4,17–18; 51:1–2,7; 32:7; 51:12–13

Isaiah 43:2

Jeremiah 29:11–12

Matthew 28:16–20

Acts 1:8

Romans 12

1 Corinthians 12

2 Corinthians 5:11–21

Ephesians 4

1 Peter 4:10–11

1 John 1:9

sonality, and spirit seemed to change before my eyes. I could tell God was working in her life. By the end of the week she was a new person. Though her work situation remained the same and she would have to face it again when she returned home, the young woman was a different person. The other participants and I knew she would make it.

At a reunion of our retreat participants six months later I saw this young woman again. The forgiveness and renewal she had experienced were more than evident as she tackled difficult issues and persons with grace and hope. I was delighted to learn she was headed for a new place of ministry and a new start. Not only had she forgiven others, she had forgiven herself.

Perhaps even more difficult for most people than forgiving another person is forgiving themselves. Most people usually suffer terrible guilt over any *transgressions, sins,* and *iniquities* (the words used by David in Psalm 32) they commit against God or another person. Guilt stabs at the heart of the person who has done something that is forbidden, failed to do what is required, twisted or perverted something that is good, projected what is false, deliberately rebelled against God, or missed the mark.

Just as it lies at the core of our forgiving others, God's forgiveness of our sins is the foundation for forgiving ourselves. God's forgiveness and self-forgiveness are all wrapped up together. Both require faith, an awareness of and acknowledgement of sin, confession, and repentance. Only then does God respond with complete forgiveness, and only then can we forgive ourselves.

Self-forgiveness is usually a very private and personal matter, between the individual and God. As such, other people do not usually know much about the experience. But the fruits of self-forgiveness may be quite evident in a person's demeanor, words, and actions. Reread the biblical accounts of David, the woman from Samaria, the woman who anointed Jesus' feet, Peter, Paul, and others who experienced forgiveness. Not only did God forgive them, but they apparently also forgave themselves. Forgiveness and its fruits are also just as evident in the lives of people today.

What Makes Me Feel Guilty?

What is guilt? Sometimes guilt is a fact and sometimes it is a feeling. Obviously we are guilty and may even feel some guilt when we commit a breach of conduct or violation of a law and receive a penalty. Guilt is a fact even if we do not feel guilty. If I exceed the speed limit while driving on a federal or state highway or county road, I have violated the law. When a state trooper or local law enforcement officer pulls me over, I am guilty and deserve the penalty of a fine. Guilt is a fact in this case. I am guilty because I have broken the law. Though I am sorry I broke the law, and even sorrier that I got caught, an act such as this one does not usually destroy my personhood or soul.

There is more to guilt than violating the civil code, however. Guilt also comes when we break God's laws and destroy fellowship with Him. We are guilty when we know we are responsible for a wrongdoing, have done something harmful, and merit condemnation or blame. Sometimes we may feel completely inadequate and begin to blame ourselves for the action, words, or attitude that causes the guilt. We experience a sense of shame at personal wrongdoing and feel responsible for a sin or wrong action, word, or attitude.

Feelings of guilt sometimes bear little or no relationship to the facts with which they are associated. We can actually feel guilty when there is no evidence that suggests a reason. In such a case there is really no reason to feel guilty. For example, a person may feel responsible for and guilt over the death of a spouse or child, perhaps feeling that if she had done more she could in some way have prevented the death. In reality, death came from a ravaged, sick body or an accident over which she had no control. A person may feel responsible for a divorce when he or she was not really at fault. Often an employee feels guilty over the decline or approaching demise of the company for which she or he works though this person is not responsible.

Guilt is a natural result of our sinful, human natures. We all fall short in our relationships with God and with others. A sense of shame results when we violate these relationships. The way we handle guilt either prolongs the pain we feel or leads to relief. The Bible usually connects guilt with sin against God or God's law. In the Old Testament sin and guilt were linked. If a person sinned, she or he was guilty. In the New Testament, however, Jesus took our sins upon Himself and provided for us a way of salvation. The Bible teaches us that each of us is responsible to God for our actions. Not only must we deal with our sin but also with the resulting guilt if we are to be whole and useful to God.

Some guilt we feel is inappropriate. For example, if I make a personal choice that God leads me to make and the choice disappoints another person, I should not feel guilty. Perhaps a person has asked me to do something and I say no because I do not believe it is the right thing for me to do. The other person is disappointed, maybe even angry with me, and tries to make me feel guilty. We cannot always meet the expectations of another person, and we do not need to carry a heavy load of guilt that another person tries to impose on us.

Some guilt we must rightfully assume, such as when we know that our words, attitudes, or actions result in a broken relationship with God or another person. Guilt is appropriate when we utter harsh words, do something hurtful to another person, or are judgmental and unforgiving. We should feel guilty when we know we have sinned and choose to remain silent with God or the person we have wronged.

In a sense, appropriate guilt is good and can be helpful. As spiritual people, guilt is a response that warns us that something we have done has caused damage to our relationship with God or with another person. The pain is God's signal to us that something is wrong and should be examined and fixed. Only when we accept responsibility for guilt and the cause from which it comes can God restore us.

Faith in God and Self

Faith, both in God and in self, is the first step in forgiving self. Essential is a belief in the love, grace, mercy, and forgiveness of God. Forgiveness is an act of God's grace and mercy and covers any and all sins. God not only forgives, but He also forgets forever and does not hold us accountable for sins we confess. "But if we confess our sins to God, he can always be trusted to forgive us and take our sins away" (1 John 1:9).

We can forgive ourselves because God forgives us. God's forgiveness erases the burden of having to live with something we have done and provides the possibility of a new and transformed life. How can we not forgive ourselves when God has already forgiven us?

We must also have faith in ourselves if we are going to be willing and able to forgive ourselves. Several important biblical truths help us when we are weighed down with sin and guilt.

First, we are made in the image of God (Gen. 1:26). This means we have a special relationship with God and responsibility to God. We can think, reason, and make choices, including the choice to forgive ourselves. Being created in God's image also means we are responsible to God for His other creation. In a sense each of us is responsible for ruling over the other creatures (Psalm 8:5–8).

Not only did God create us in His image, He knows everything about us (Psalm 139). He formed or put us together in our mothers' bodies. His creative act is miraculous and wonderful (Psalm 139:13–14). Because God so carefully created us, He has cared about us since the day we were conceived and continues to care each day of our lives. God created each of us like we are, with the personalities, gifts, skills, and abilities we have.

God gives spiritual gifts to each of us to use in His service through the church (1 Cor. 12; Rom. 12; Eph. 4; 1 Peter 4:10–11). We are valuable to God. He wants us to use these gifts and abilities for His good and His benefit. He wants us to serve and to minister for Him in such a way to build up His kingdom. How can we do this when we are burdened down with guilt and refuse to forgive ourselves?

Finally, God has a plan for our lives. He knew His plan for us even before we were born (Psalm 139:16*b*). God's overall plan for the world is huge and all encompassing, but each of us fits into it. Even as He had a plan for His chosen people in the Old Testament, He has a plan for each individual today. He expressed it this way to His chosen people and we, too, can claim this promise: "I will bless you with a future filled with hope—a future of success, not of suffering. You will turn back to me and ask for help, and I will answer your prayers" (Jer. 29:11–12).

When we accept Jesus Christ as Savior and Lord, God makes us into new creatures with a responsibility to be reconcilers and to bring other people to Him (2 Cor. 5:11–21). He commissions us to take His message of good news to all people everywhere (Matt. 28:16–20;

Acts 1:8). Unresolved guilt and unconfessed, unforgiven sin impede our participation in God's kingdom work. We are empty vessels when we cannot or will not forgive ourselves.

When my late husband and I were experiencing grief and difficulty over his declining health and loss of his ministry, he reminded me time and again that God was not through with us yet. An avid baseball fan, his most common expression was, "I think it is time for our faith to stand up at the plate and go to bat." That reminder was so true as he found new avenues of ministry from our home and his wheelchair. I also found new avenues of service as one who had been through the deep rivers and the fire (Isa. 43:2). God proved over and over that He was not through with us yet but still had plans for our lives. Life or forgiveness of self is not always easy, but God provides the will, the stamina, the faith, the courage, and the ability to keep us going and serving.

How can a person not forgive self when she or he is made in the image of God? Is a miraculous and wonderful creation? Has spiritual gifts and special abilities that can be used in God's service? Knows that God has a plan for her or his life?

Accepting Responsibility

Faith is the first step in forgiving self. Accepting responsibility and being accountable for wrong words, attitudes, or actions marks the next. Both sin and feelings of guilt are serious matters we must acknowledge before forgiveness can occur. Unresolved guilt results in a paralyzed spirit. But when we accept responsibility for our sin and guilt and ask for and receive forgiveness from God, we are absolved of sin and guilt. God has promised that He will forgive our sin when we confess it (1 John 1:9). He will also take away guilt and give us the desire and ability to forgive ourselves. Accepting responsibility and acknowledging accountability are keys to the process of forgiving self.

David, the Old Testament king, wrote two beautiful prayers about his sin, guilt, and forgiveness. Psalm 51, a prayer for forgiveness, came when the prophet Nathan confronted him after he committed adultery with Bathsheba. It was his plea for mercy, forgiveness, and cleansing. Psalm 32 is David's expression of the joy forgiveness brings. Forgiveness of self also brings joy and restored fellowship with God and other persons.

David first acknowledged the seriousness of his sins and accepted responsibility for them. Through nobody's fault but his own did he sin. Psalm 51 is a bitter lament of his deep feelings of remorse and repentance. David was truly sorry for his adultery with Bathsheba and for murdering her husband Uriah to cover up his sin. He knew his actions had hurt many people.

"I know about my sins, and I cannot forget my terrible guilt. You are really the one I have sinned against; I have disobeyed you and have done wrong. So it is right and fair for you to correct and punish me. I have sinned and done wrong since the day I was born. But you want complete honesty, so teach me true wisdom" (Psalm 51:3–6).

Psalm 38 reveals David as a sinner who is suffering and weighed down with sin and guilt. His guilt was a burden and he expresses his grief and anxiety to God.

"My body hurts all over because of your anger. Even my bones are in pain, and my sins are so heavy that I am crushed. . . . I am about to collapse from constant pain. I told you my sins, and I am sorry for them" (Psalm 38:3–4,17–18).

David felt like most of us feel when we have done wrong and are burdened with guilt. He acknowledged his sins and took full responsibility for them, a necessary step in the process of healing and forgiveness.

Confession and Repentance

After we have been honest before God and have acknowledged the seriousness of our sins, we must follow this with confession and repentance. This act of faith is not easy. Notice how David handled this important step in Psalm 51.

"You are kind, God! Please have pity on me. You are always merciful! Please wipe away my sins. Wash me clean from all of my sin and guilt.... Wash me with hyssop [a small bush with bunches of small, white flowers used to sprinkle blood or water in various ceremonies, here used to symbolize being cleansed from sin¹] until I am clean and whiter than snow" (Psalm 51:1–2,7).

God has assured us that He forgives our sins when we confess and repent. He takes away and wipes out sin and lifts the burden of guilt. He cancels the debts. In Psalm 32 David expresses the joy of forgiveness. He calls God his hiding place and protector, and says God puts songs in his heart (Psalm 32:7).

Repentance must come alongside of or be simultaneous with confession. Repentance indicates our willingness to turn from our sins and to serve God. David expressed his repentance this way: "Make me as happy as you did when you saved me; make me want to obey! I will teach sinners your Law, and they will return to you" (Psalm 51:12–13).

Prayer, confession, and repentance are all necessary steps in seeking God's forgiveness and in forgiving ourselves. We cannot handle self-forgiveness alone. We need God's help.

Results of Forgiving Self

When we forgive ourselves, we experience joy, peace, spiritual health, and a restored relationship. Our guilt burden is lifted, and we are cleansed and whole again.

We can once again be useful to God. Though we can never forget our sins, we have the assurance that God forgets. We remember forever the kindness God shows us in forgiving, forgetting, and allowing us to move on with our lives for His sake.

Questions for Thought and Discussion

1. Why is it so difficult for us to forgive ourselves? How is self-forgiveness wrapped up in God's forgiveness?

2. Describe an experience when you had trouble forgiving yourself. How were grace and mercy evident to you? How did you finally experience forgiveness? How did the situation turn out? What were the fruits of forgiveness?

3. What does guilt mean to you and do to you? When is guilt not appropriate? When it is appropriate?

4. How does your faith in God help you in forgiving yourself?

5. How does faith in yourself help in forgiving yourself? What helps you to be able to forgive yourself? How do you feel before you do? How do you feel afterwards?

6. Have you ever felt like David because of your sin and guilt? What did you do about it? How did you express your feelings?

7. Why are prayer, confession, and repentance necessary steps in forgiving self?

8. What have been the results in situations where you have forgiven yourself? What about others you have

known about? How does forgiveness of self affect one's usefulness in God's kingdom?

---

[1] *The Learning Bible*, Contemporary English Version (New York: American Bible Society, 2000), 1046.

11

What Does Prayer Have to Do with Forgiveness?

Prayer and forgiveness are two sides of the same coin and complement each other in God's will for all of us.

Especially in the teachings of Jesus we find a strong connection between forgiveness and prayer. Forgiveness enables prayer to work; conversely, unwillingness to forgive blocks effective prayer. Forgiveness, or the lack of forgiveness, also bears a relationship to other Christian disciplines such as meditation, fasting, study, lifestyle, service, and worship.

One young woman I know strongly illustrates this connection. The daughter of a minister, she grew up in a Christian home, was active in her church, and did all of the things a growing Christian usually does. Bright, gifted, and talented, her college graduation led to a promising career, and a new marriage signaled a great life ahead.

1 Chronicles 21:8

2 Chronicles; 1; 5:13–14; 7:1–2; 7:11; 7:14

Psalms 51; 32; 38

Matthew 6; 6:5–15; 6:5–9; 6:9; 6:10; 6:11–13; 6:14–15

Mark 11:12–14; 11:22–26

Luke 11; 23:34

John 13; 16; 13:34–35; 14–16; 17; 17:20–26

Acts 6:8; 7:59; 1:8; 6:5; 8:18–19; 8:15–17; 8:20; 8:21–23; 8:25; 6–7

Ephesians 4:32

After only a year, however, the marriage failed, the result of abuse. Feeling responsible for the divorce and taking a huge load of guilt upon herself, she temporarily withdrew from those who loved her most. Then things again looked bright as her career progressed. She found someone else with whom to share her life, and she and her second husband had three wonderful children.

Though it does not seem possible or fair that tragedy would strike again, this marriage also failed as a result of abuse, finally ending in divorce. The young woman, though surrounded by a loving support system, her children, and a good job, again fell into despair and assumed another load of guilt. Where had she failed? What had she done wrong? If she had not gotten out of shape physically or suffered from a debilitating illness, would the marriage have worked?

Time and her deep commitment to the Lord eventually prevailed. She spent countless hours thinking, reflecting, and praying to come to terms with what happened, especially this time. Because she lived in an area blessed with many rivers and bays and the beauty of God's creation, she could easily view God's majesty and the bigness of His world. As she looked at the water time and time again she began to see her problems as small in comparison to God's greatness. She realized that if God could forgive her, she certainly needed to forgive herself. She reasoned that dwelling on past mistakes is probably one of Satan's greatest devices for keeping a person distracted from the direction God wants them to go. The prayers of her soul included confession, a contrite heart, and finally, forgiveness from her Lord.

Though no one knew the deep stirrings of this young woman's soul, the outward fruits of forgiveness became evident. One day she seemed to make a turn. She began taking care of herself, working on her appearance, spending quality time with her family, and again engaging in the life and activities of her church. God truly brings forgiveness when we come to Him with prayerful hearts.

Jesus, an Incredible Example

Jesus' Sermon on the Mount includes a primary principle about forgiveness. Read the Model Prayer as recorded in Matthew 6 and Luke 11.

In the Sermon on the Mount (Matt. 5–7), Jesus taught His followers about character, influence, conduct, and destiny. In short, He taught us what it means to live as one of His followers, practical things we encounter in daily life. The Model Prayer, usually called the Lord's Prayer, is part of a larger section about prayer in Matthew 6:5–15.

Prayer is an attitude as much as an act, according to Jesus. It is as much what we feel as it is what we say. It is a private matter, between an individual and God, and can happen anytime, anywhere. Jesus warned us against praying in order to be seen by others. People who do this, Jesus said, are hypocrites (Matt. 6:5–9), or show-offs.[1]

Jesus followed these words with the Model Prayer (Matt. 6:9–13), a pattern for the prayers of a Christ follower. Notice first the petitions in this prayer that acknowledge God's glory. Followers of Christ must recognize God as their spiritual Father in heaven and realize He is the one and only God. Believers are to praise God (Matt. 6:9), let God reign in their lives, and submit to Him. "Come and set up your kingdom so that everyone on earth will obey you" (Matt. 6:10). God's spiritual kingdom is present as Christ reigns in the hearts of His followers.

God provides for Christ followers and leads them along the way so they will not fall into temptation. "Give us our food for today. Forgive us for doing wrong as we forgive others. Keep us from being tempted and protect us from evil" (Matt. 6:11–13).

The Model Prayer clearly deals with forgiveness. Jesus instructed believers to pray for forgiveness for doing wrong *as they forgive others*. He then amplified this part of the Model Prayer, the only part where He did so. "If you forgive others for the wrongs they do to you, your Father in heaven will forgive you. But if you don't forgive others, your Father will not forgive your sins" (Matt. 6:14–15).

Jesus made it clear that we cannot ask for ourselves what we deny others. If we refuse to forgive others, God will also refuse to forgive us. New Testament teachings instruct Christ followers to "be kind and compassionate to one another, forgiving each other, just as in Christ God forgave you" (Eph. 4:32 NIV). God acted in love when He sent His Son to die for our sins. We, too, must act in love to one another. This act of love includes forgiveness.

A fig tree Jesus spied in the distance became the vehicle for conveying an important spiritual truth. As they were traveling, Jesus became hungry. Spotting the fig tree, they went to see whether it had any figs. It did not, and Jesus put a curse on the tree (Mark 11:12–14). The next morning as the group again passed the tree, the disciples noted that it was completely dried up. Jesus took this opportunity to teach them:

"Have faith in God! If you have faith in God and don't doubt, you can tell this mountain to get up and jump into the sea, and it will. Everything you ask for in prayer will be yours, if you only have faith. Whenever you stand up to pray, <u>you must forgive what others have done to you</u>. *Then your Father in heaven will forgive your sins" (Mark 11:22–26, author's emphasis).*

In a real sense, forgiveness is the cornerstone of our relationship with God. God forgives our sins; therefore, we can and must forgive those who wrong us. If we do not forgive, how can we say we understand the meaning of Christ's forgiveness? We must treat others as God treats us.

Not only is forgiveness key to our relationship with God, prayer is the key to forgiveness. Certainly it is easier to ask God for forgiveness than it is to grant forgiveness to others. But as we pray for forgiveness for ourselves, we must also pray for the grace and mercy to forgive others.

Prayers for Forgiveness

The Gospel writers provide the beautiful example of Jesus praying for the forgiveness of those who put Him to death. Our Savior links prayer and forgiveness. "Father, forgive these people! They don't know what they're doing" (Luke 23:34). He asked God to forgive the Jewish leaders, the Roman politicians and soldiers, and the bystanders at the Cross. He prayed for the people who were His detractors throughout His public ministry, ending in His crucifixion.

Many parallels exist between the death of Stephen and the death of Christ. Stephen was chosen as a deacon, along with six others, to help with the perceived problem of unequal distribution of food to the widows in the early church. In the Book of Acts, Luke describes Stephen as "full of grace and power" and doing "great wonders and signs among the people" (Acts 6:8). But living out his Christian faith got Stephen into trouble. His powerful witness for his Lord before the Jewish council led to his death by stoning. As Stephen was being stoned, he knelt down and called out in a loud voice: "Lord, don't blame them for what they have done" (Acts 7:59). Instead of railing against his tormentors, Stephen prayed for forgiveness for them, even as Jesus did for His tormentors as He died.

As we have seen in earlier chapters, David's prayers are also closely related to forgiveness. Many of David's writings read like a journal. Psalm 51 expresses the terrible condition of the unforgiven sinner. David asked to be washed clean and given a pure heart and steadfast spirit. He acknowledged that he was sinful by nature and expressed his grief and sorrow at being separated from God. He acknowledged his guilt. Only through the grace and mercy of God could David find peace and forgiveness.

Psalm 32 records David's prayer of thanksgiving for how forgiveness brings true joy. God gives real happiness and relief from guilt only when we personally ask Him to forgive our sins. In Psalm 38, David expressed his belief that God alone is the true source of healing and protection for those who confess their sins to him.

Not only did David confess his sins and pray for forgiveness after his acts of adultery and murder, he also acknowledged his sins and asked for forgiveness when he took a census against God's will. God was angry with David and punished Israel. David prayed, "I am your servant. But what I did was stupid and terribly wrong. Please forgive me" (1 Chron. 21:8).

Prayer as a Condition for Forgiveness

During the times of the kings, the nation of Israel was notorious for falling away from God and turning to idols. Time and time again, God had to bring them back to Himself. By reminding the Israelites of their past, the writer of the second book of Chronicles hoped to bring them back to God.

Written to unify the nation around the true and proper worship of God, 2 Chronicles helped the people remember events from the past during the reign of Solomon, David's son, up to the beginning of Babylonian captivity.

The writer emphasized the building of the Temple and its importance.

Solomon's reign was one of peace and prosperity. The people who returned from exile in Babylonia needed to hear these stories.[2] When Solomon became king, he asked for and received wisdom (2 Chron. 1). His greatest achievement was building the Temple. During the dedication of the Temple God demonstrated His presence in powerful ways. A cloud filled the temple and God's glory was in the cloud. The light was so bright that the priests could not finish their work. Fire came down from heaven and burned up the offerings, and again God's glory filled the Temple (2 Chron. 5:13–14; 7:1–2). Solomon and the people worshiped God. Solomon's great work was finished (2 Chron. 7:11).

The Lord appeared to Solomon in a dream and gave the conditions for forgiveness, conditions which included prayer: "If my own people will humbly pray and turn back to me and stop sinning, then I will answer them from heaven. I will forgive them and make their land fertile once again" (2 Chron. 7:14).

God set forth four conditions for forgiveness: humbling self and admitting sin, praying to God for forgiveness, seeking God continually, and turning from sinful behavior. Repentance involves changed behavior.

Jesus' High Priestly Prayer

Nearing the end of His life and with His public ministry drawing to a close, Jesus spent His last week on earth preparing His followers, especially the 12 apostles, for the days ahead. John recorded much of this preparation in his Gospel account. Sometimes Jesus' teachings here are called His farewell discourses. He taught His disciples in the upper room at His Last Supper with them, and He taught them on the way to Gethsemane. Jesus was preparing His disciples to carry on without His physical presence. These instructions seem just as appropriate for modern-day disciples.

Read chapters 13–16 from John's Gospel. Notice the progression of events during that week. Jesus washed His disciples' feet, observed the Last Supper with them, responded to Peter's declaration of allegiance by predicting his denials, told what would happen to Him, and gave the disciples a new command (John 13). "But I am giving you a new command. You must love each other, just as I have loved you. If you love each other, everyone will know that you are my disciples" (John 13:34–35). Somehow I think Jesus' command to love one another also implies forgiveness.

Jesus taught that He is the way to the Father and promised the Holy Spirit. He described Himself as the True Vine and God as the Gardener and told about the world's hatred. He taught about the work of the Holy Spirit and that sorrow will turn to joy (John 14–16).

At the end of His discourses, Jesus prayed what is usually called His high priestly prayer (see John 17), so named because Jesus assumes the role of the high priest in interceding for the people and becoming a sacrifice for their sins.[3] Jesus prayed for Himself, for His immediate disciples who would be left in the world after He ascended to the Father, and for all Christ followers, including you and me.

Though Jesus' prayer for believers did not specifically mention forgiveness, He prayed for unity of purpose among believers based on their unity with Him and the Father. He prayed for their powerful witness of His love so the world would believe that God sent Him. These believers, which include us today, would continue and extend His ministry. Forgiveness is necessary for unity and is an outgrowth of love.

"*I am not praying just for these followers* [his immediate

disciples]. *I am also praying for everyone else who will have faith because of what my followers will say about me. I want all of them to be one with each other, just as I am one with you and you are one with me. I also want them to be one with us. Then the people of this world will believe that you sent me.*

"I have honored my followers in the same way that you honored me, in order that they may be one with each other, just as we are one. I am one with them, and you are one with me, so that they may become completely one. Then this world's people will know that you sent me. They will know that you love my followers as much as you love me.

"Father, I want everyone you have given me to be with me, wherever I am. Then they will see the glory that you have given me, because you loved me before the world was created. Good Father, the people of this world don't know you. But I know you, and my followers know that you sent me. I told them what you are like, and I will tell them even more. Then the love that you have for me will become part of them and I will be one with them" (John 17:20–26).

Prayer for forgiveness and the act of forgiveness seem necessary for unity and an ongoing witness.

The Only Way to God's Power

Acts 8 records the account of Philip preaching in Samaria and teaches that the only way to receive God's power is to turn from sin, ask God for forgiveness, accept Christ as Savior, and then be filled with the Holy Spirit. Persecution, most recently the stoning of Stephen, had forced the Christians out of Jerusalem into Judea and Samaria. As these believers took the gospel with them and shared it with non-Jews, they were fulfilling the middle part of Acts 1:8.

Philip, who was one of seven deacons chosen to help with the distribution of food in the early church (Acts 6:5), went to the city of Samaria where he preached the gospel and performed miracles of healing and casting out demons. Samaria, the region between Galilee to the north and Judea to the south, was the same region where Jesus had the redemptive encounter with the woman at the well. The Orthodox Jews and Samaritans, whom the Jews considered half-breeds, hated each other. Nevertheless, Jesus commanded His followers to spread the gospel there (Acts 1:8).

Reaching the Samaritans was probably not a problem for Philip. As a Hellenized, or Greek-oriented, Jew, he may have grown up outside of Palestine. Jews who had been exposed to Greek culture seemed more open to understanding the universality of the gospel.[4]

Simon then entered the story. A local resident who had long practiced witchcraft or magic, he was able to call up the spirits of the dead and tell fortunes. Though Simon believed what Philip taught and was baptized, he later tried to buy the gift of the Holy Spirit from Peter and John (Acts 8:18–19).

When the apostles in Jerusalem heard what was happening in Samaria and how the people were accepting the word of God, they sent Peter and John to investigate. Perhaps it was hard for these Jews to believe that Samaritans could truly become Christ followers. The Jewish Christians were still not sure Gentiles and half-Jews could receive the Holy Spirit (Acts 8:14). Peter and John found true believers in Samaria, but these believers had not yet received the Holy Spirit. They prayed that the believing, baptized Samaritans would be given the Holy Spirit. Then they laid their hands on everyone who believed in Jesus Christ and the people received the Holy Spirit (Acts 8:15–17).

Peter and John's action was unusual. Believers normally receive the Holy Spirit at the moment of their conversion. Perhaps no one had told these Samaritans about the Holy Spirit. Obviously this part of the Christian experience was missing from their group. When Peter told them about the Holy Spirit, however, the news must have electrified their hearts.[5]

When Simon noticed that the Holy Spirit was given only when the apostles placed their hands on the people, he had an idea that might enhance his practice of magic. He offered money to Peter and John, trying to buy this power and bestow the gift himself (Acts 8:18–19). Peter rebuked Simon in no uncertain terms. "You and your money will both end up in hell if you think you can buy God's gift!" (Acts 8:20). God's power came only one way. A person must repent of her or his sins, ask God for forgiveness, and accept Christ as Savior. Only then would that person receive the Holy Spirit. Paul told Simon: "You don't have any part in this, and God sees that your heart isn't right. Get rid of these evil thoughts and ask God to forgive you. I can see that you are jealous and bound by your evil ways" (Acts 8:21–23).

Simon immediately asked Peter to pray for him, that these things would not happen to him. Scripture does not mention Simon again, but an adaptation of his name, "simony," was given to the practice of religion for money. The gospel continued to spread after this experience. Peter and John preached the gospel to many Samaritan villages on their way home (Acts 8:25).

Prayer and forgiveness are indeed inseparably linked today. Forgiveness cannot come without prayer. Since prayer is an attitude and not an act and involves both talking with God and listening to God, it is not always audible. One can be in a spirit and attitude of prayer that leads to forgiveness—forgiveness from God for sins, forgiveness of others for wrongs they have committed, and forgiveness of self.

Questions for Thought and Discussion

1. Why do you think prayer and forgiveness are inseparably linked? Can you pray without asking for forgiveness and help with forgiving others? Can you forgive without the foundation of prayer?

2. What does Jesus' prayer for forgiveness for those who put Him to death teach you about forgiving those who have wronged you? How can you put this attitude of forgiving prayer into practice in your life?

3. Describe the situation in which the church leader Stephen found himself in Acts 6–7. Have you ever been in a similar situation? How did Stephen stand up for Jesus? How did the people who heard him react? How did Stephen act in this difficult situation? What does his example mean to us today? Where does our wisdom and strength come from today?

4. Have you had a personal experience of confessing your sins and receiving forgiveness in addition to your initial conversion experience? How did it make you feel? How did you express your feelings? What kind of change was evident in your life?

5. Read John 13–16. What is Jesus teaching you in these chapters? How do these teachings apply to your mission of taking the good news about Jesus to the whole world?

6. Where is God's temple today? What are the conditions for forgiveness for these "temples"?

7. How does it feel to know Jesus prayed for you? How can unity and love be applied today in carrying out your witness for Christ to the world?

8. What does forgiveness have to do with the power of the Holy Spirit?

9. What evidence have you seen of the connection between prayer and forgiveness? Personally? In the lives of others?

---

[1] *The Learning Bible*, Contemporary English Version (New York: American Bible Society, 2000), 1748.
[2] Ibid., 777–78; *Life Application Study Bible*, New International Version (Wheaton, IL: Tyndale House Publishers, Inc., 1991), 712–13.
[3] James E. Carter, *Layman's Bible Book Commentary* (Nashville: Broadman Press, 1984), 18:122.
[4] Robert L. Maddox Jr., *Layman's Bible Book Commentary* (Nashville: Broadman Press, 1979), 19:54.
[5] Ibid., 55.

12

How Can I Live a Forgiven Life?

After receiving God's forgiveness as an act of grace and mercy, get guidance from God's Word, and commit yourself to do God's will in Christ.

Candy (not her real name) made a religious vow as a young woman and embarked on a life journey in a church-related vocation. A while later, she fell desperately in love and left her vows for marriage to and a new life with Jim (not his real name). For quite some time the young couple was happy and things went well in their new relationship. Candy and Jim established their home in such a way that allowed Candy to stay at home with their three daughters. But, Jim had straying eyes and a straying heart. He left Candy and the girls for another woman and moved in with her close to his former home.

Isaiah 40:21–28; 40:29–31

Matthew 5–7; 15:18–20; 22:37–39; 5:1–12; 5:13–16; 5:17–20; 5:21–26; 5:27–30; 5:31–32; 5:33–37; 5:38–42; 5:43–48; 6:1–4; 6:5–15; 6:16–18; 6:19–24; 6:25–34; 7:1–6; 7:7–12; 7:13–14; 7:15–20; 7:21–29; 28:18–20; 8:28–34

Mark 16:14–18

Luke 15:7,10,24,32; 6:45; 24:36–49

John 20:19–23

Romans 1–11; 12–15; 15:7; 13:8 to 15:6

1 Corinthians 10:12–13

2 Corinthians 5:17–19

Galatians 6:1–10

Ephesians 4–6; 2:8–10; 6:10–18; 3:14–21

Life became hard for Candy as is often true for an abandoned spouse and single parent. Forced by her circumstances to earn some money and with rusty work-world skills, Candy took a job in a small company's shipping department. Jim was not really satisfied either. Something kept tugging at his heart and he missed Candy and his daughters tremendously. After 5 years of separation, Jim had the courage and latent love to ask Candy to forgive and take him back.

Philippians; 3:12–14
Colossians 1:10; 1:13–14; 3–4
Hebrews 12:1–2

Though this was not an easy choice for Candy, she had strong love and courage too. Candy demonstrated complete forgiveness of Jim and their relationship was restored, not to what it had been before, but to something new. Candy exhibited an incredible love, respect, and care for Jim. She showed no animosity toward Jim and even displayed renewed trust in him. Apparently Candy had the ability to let go of any negative emotions she had felt or of guilt and accusations. The restored marriage has stood the test for a number of years since Jim's repentance and Candy's forgiveness. And, though Jim travels regularly in his job and is often away from home, mutual trust exists between this couple.

Candy's model of forgiveness not only to Jim but also to her fellow employees has been a testimony to what living a forgiven life really means. She now heads the shipping department and influences others daily. Her co-workers say Candy exhibits the spirit of forgiveness, a presence of love, and the demonstration of what it means to follow Christ. She seems to draw hurting people to herself. In a sense she is the corporate "mother" at her workplace as she gives strength, peace, and love in abundance. She has only positive things to say about Jim and their life together. One fellow worker describes Candy as intelligent, approachable, and close to God with an inner strength and peace. She is perceived as spiritual, but not "religious."

Forgiveness for Christ followers results in restored, rebuilt, transformed lives and relationships, both with God and with others such as Candy demonstrates. While the personal healing that comes with forgiveness is a wonderful benefit, forgiveness also leads Christian believers into a new lifestyle and way of life. Receiving and granting forgiveness enabled Candy not only to love her family in a new way, but also to live out a Christian lifestyle among her fellow workers. Through forgiveness God in His grace and mercy lifts and takes away the burden of guilt, hides the sins, and cancels the debts. How can a person who has experienced such grace and mercy not live for God?

When we are forgiven, we have a renewed and vibrant fellowship with God and other people. Luke 15's accounts of the lost sheep, the lost coin, and the lost son remind us of God's happiness and joy in heaven when we turn back to Him (Luke 15:7,10,24,32). Without God's ongoing gift of forgiveness, a Christian's life would continue to be full of guilt. But forgiveness cleanses and restores.

Store shelves are lined with countless books and study materials, and seminars and conferences abound about living life as a follower of Christ. Our purpose in these pages is to examine biblical principles of forgiveness as an act of grace and mercy rather than delve into the entirety of what a Christ follower's life should be like. But a closer look at some biblical guidance on how to live a forgiven life can be helpful.

Living a Kingdom Life

Jesus came to earth to begin His kingdom, a spiritual kingdom that will be fully realized only when He comes again. He died for all people to free them from sin's oppression and to fulfill God's plan of forgiveness. Anyone, regardless of race, sex, nationality or people group, economic status or past sins, can enter and be a part of this kingdom through faith. When a person believes in Jesus Christ as Savior and Lord, her or his life is completely transformed to do Christ's kingdom work. This is living the forgiven life.

We find guidance on how to live a forgiven life and be kingdom people in God's Word. For example, Jesus' Sermon on the Mount, recorded in Matthew 5–7 with some parts repeated throughout the Gospels, is His keynote address on what it really means to be His follower. This sermon or discourse is a dissertation on the practicalities of the Christian life. Jesus teaches His followers how to live, not only through His words, but also through His actions. His expectations of His followers are extremely high and His demands rigorous.

Obedience to Christ characterizes the heart of a woman or man who seeks to live a forgiven life. Rather than following rules and regulations, it instead involves one's attitude and actions (Matt. 15:18–20). According to Jesus, "good people do good things because of the good in their hearts. . . . Your words show what is in your heart" (Luke 6:45). The essence of the forgiven life is love, both complete love for our heavenly Father and love for fellow human beings. God's Word identifies for us the two most important commandments: *"Love the Lord your God with all your heart, soul, and mind. This is the first and most important commandment. The second most important commandment is like this one. And it is, 'Love others as much as you love yourself'" (Matt. 22:37–39).*

The practical implications of Jesus' teachings in the Sermon on the Mount about living the forgiven life are extensive. Just take a look at the headings for these chapters in several different translations of the Bible. The *Life Application Study Bible*, a study Bible for the New International Version translation, provides a succinct and well-organized outline. And, *The Learning Bible*, based on the Contemporary English Version translation, gives a simple outline of His teachings. The following paragraphs are a combination of these two listings and include brief summaries of Jesus' teachings about living as a Christ follower[1] It all comes from an obedient heart and a life filled with love. What did Jesus really have to say to us about life in His Sermon on the Mount?

Blessings (Matt. 5:1–12)

The Beatitudes teach us how to have real and lasting happiness and describe what a person should be like as a Christ follower, a person who is blessed because she or he is part of the kingdom of God. The kingdom life is a life of hope and real joy, guided by God's standards rather than the world's standards. As a result, our lives should demonstrate hope and joy. The life of a Christ follower is not necessarily a life of ease, fame, or fortune. It may well involve sadness and sorrow, hunger and pain, even persecution. It is a life, however, of loving, giving, serving, and helping. Kingdom values that are eternal are more important than earthly values that are temporary. In order to be truly blessed with hope, joy, and real happiness, we must follow Christ and His teachings fully.

Salt and Light (Matt. 5:13–16)

Jesus says that Christians are like salt and light to the world. Even as salt gives flavor and keeps something from spoiling, thus adding value, a Christ follower exerts a positive influence in the world, giving flavor and meaning to the lives of others. We also radiate light from within, dispelling the darkness, standing up for what is right, and speaking out to show others what Christ is like.

The Law of Moses (Matt. 5:17–20)
Jesus did not come to do away with Old Testament law and prophecy, but to fulfill them. He brought a higher righteousness and a new standard for living. The life of a forgiven person is a life of righteousness that knows no legal limits. It stands opposite to a life that is bound by rules and regulations. A Christ follower lives as one changed or transformed from the inside out, with new attitudes and actions. The rest of the Sermon on the Mount spells out some teachings about higher righteousness.

Anger (Matt. 5:21–26)
Anger, hatred, and bitterness have no place in the life of a Christian. These attitudes are sin because they are the direct opposites of love, God's standard for the forgiven life. Anger is a dangerous emotion and can get out of control if left unchecked. Anger can destroy relationships. Jesus taught His followers to practice self-control in attitudes and actions, resolve problems, settle differences, make peace, and restore fellowship. Reconciliation with others shows a right relationship with God.

Lust (Matt. 5:27–30)
Faithfulness in marriage is the only way for followers of Christ. Both adultery and lust are wrong and sinful. Lust, the seed for sinful intentions or thoughts, is usually the beginning point for adultery. Self-control and self-discipline help free us from lust.

Divorce (Matt. 5:31–32)
God intends for marriage to be a lifetime commitment. Divorce is harmful and destructive. Jesus raised the position of women and marriage to a new high. Marriage is a permanent commitment, not a temporary contract or relationship. This is the ideal for a Christ follower. Yet when we fail to reach the ideal, we can still experience

God's forgiveness. God forgives when we confess our sins and shortcomings, and we, too, can forgive a broken relationship with God's help.

Promises (Matt. 5:33–37)
Followers of Christ are truthful and keep their word. Keeping promises builds trust and makes committed relationships possible.

Revenge (Matt. 5:38–42)
Mercy, not revenge or retaliation, is the appropriate response for a Christ follower. This represents a higher standard of righteousness than one's usual and natural behavior. Rather than getting even with another person or taking matters into our own hands, we deliberately choose to do good to those who wrong us, pray for them, love them, and forgive them. The principle is generosity rather than retaliation.

Loving Enemies (Matt. 5:43–48)
Followers of Christ also have a higher standard in relating to enemies. Though it is not easy to love and forgive those who have wronged us, we show our love for God when we do, because God's Word tells us we are to love our enemies and pray for those who persecute us, even when we don't feel like doing so.

Giving to the Needy (Matt. 6:1–4)
Rather than seeking recognition or adulation for what we do, we ought to help others in practical and secret ways. Showing God's love, grace, and mercy by giving and ministering to others should be our only motivation.

Prayer (Matt. 6:5–15)
Prayer is private and personal communication between God and us, not a public display. God, not other people,

is our audience. Jesus taught that it is wrong to pray just so others will see us. A Christ follower prays out of a sincere heart, seeking God's will for her or his life. Notice Jesus' warning about forgiveness here; if we do not forgive others, neither will God forgive us.

Fasting (Matt. 6:16–18)
Fasting is a practice of going without food in order to spend time in prayer. It can be a helpful spiritual discipline for Christians, but it too must come from the proper motive. Fasting involves an act of quiet, sincere, self-sacrifice, not a public act to achieve human praise or gain public approval. It is between a believer and God.

Money (Matt. 6:19–24)
Our hearts tend to follow those things we most value. For this reason it is dangerous to make the accumulation of things our life's goal. God will guide us as we make decisions about the use of money and possessions. God must be our master, not money or material possessions. Rather than storing up earthly accumulations, Jesus encouraged His followers to store up treasures in heaven—loving deeds of service and worship. We worship and serve what or who is most important to us.

Worry (Matt. 6:25–34)
God promises to supply all our needs (Phil. 4:19). Since that is the case, why should we worry about material things? Worry can immobilize and destroy our effectiveness. We show our faith in God when we rely on Him rather than ourselves. God knows all of our needs, so worry wastes time and energy and demonstrates a lack of faith.

Criticizing Others (Matt. 7:1–6)
A hypocritical, judgmental attitude is destructive to both

the believer and to those who are criticized or judged. Jesus warned us against judging, condemning, or criticizing others and instead reminded us to become aware of our own faults instead.

Asking, Seeking, and Knocking (Matt. 7:7–12)
When we pray, we indicate that we have faith that God will answer. Jesus teaches us to seek God with persistent faith and not give up. Our persistence does not necessarily mean we will get what we ask for, but we can be assured that God will answer our prayers.

The Way to Heaven (Matt. 7:13–14)
There is only one way to live eternally with God: believe in Jesus Christ as Savior and Lord. Not everyone chooses this narrow way, yet it is the only way to heaven.

Fruit in People's Lives (Matt. 7:15–20)
God evaluates our lives by the "fruits" we produce, or how we live out the forgiven life. Each of us must make choices about how we will live. While the narrow way is difficult, it is the only way for the Christ follower. Living as a kingdom person according to God's standards involves self-discipline, sacrifice, and love. Our guide is God's Word and how it instructs us to live.

Two Builders (Matt. 7:21–29)
Only when we build our lives on the strong foundation of God's teachings will we find happiness and fulfillment. As followers of Christ, our lives reflect discipleship, obedience to God, and service to Him and others.

Proper Relationships and Treatment of Others

By living in right relationships with others and treating

other people with dignity and respect, we show that we belong to Christ. God's Word, especially Paul's writings, gives practical guidelines about how followers of Christ should live. Even though the Apostle Paul portrays lofty ideals and high standards, he in no way minimizes the challenge of the Christian life.

The good news of the gospel is saving faith for all people (Rom. 1–11). By following Christ and obeying God's Word, believers are equipped to deal with important issues such as obeying authorities, love, Christ's return, criticism of and causing problems for other persons, pleasing others, and the good news being for all people (Rom. 12–15). Forgiveness is key to the proper life of a forgiven person: "Honor God by accepting each other, as Christ has accepted you" (Rom. 15:7).

Believers are to do good to all people and help one another (Gal. 6:1–10). God's Word provides standards for how believers are to live as the body of Christ, the Church (Eph. 4–6). Because of what God has done for us, we need to live lives that honor Him, please Him by doing good deeds, and come to know Him even better (Col. 1:10). Why? We do so because of His forgiveness. "God rescued us from the dark power of Satan and brought us into the kingdom of his dear Son, who forgives our sins and sets us free" (Col 1:13–14). And, we must understand what our new life in Christ means and how it affects the way we live in fellowship with one another (Col. 3–4). The Christian life should be a life of joy (Phil.).

Most of us fear falling into temptation at any time, even though we know God forgives. God's Word gives us this assurance:

"Even if you think you can stand up to temptation, be careful not to fall. You are tempted in the same way that everyone else is tempted. But God can be trusted not to let you be tempted too much, and he will show you how

to escape from your temptations" (1 Cor. 10:12–13).

Jesus Christ brings unity and peace to His followers because God gives them His gift of salvation and forgiveness through His grace and mercy.

"You were saved by faith in God, who treats us much better than we deserve. This is God's gift to you, and not anything you have done on your own. It isn't something you have earned, so there is nothing you can brag about. God planned for us to do good things and to live as he has always wanted us to live. That's why he sent Christ to make us what we are" (Eph. 2:8–10).

Understanding All of God's Word

Both studying and reading the Bible are major disciplines in the life of a Christ follower. It is our guide on how to live the forgiven life. Though we learn much about expectations for a believer's life from the New Testament, God uses the entirety of the Bible to change our lives. By reading God's Word regularly and systematically, we gain strength for the day and guidance for living the Christian life.

I have found it helpful to read the Bible through each year in a different translation. A revered Bible scholar and respected co-worker gave me a plan a number of years ago for doing this. He suggested putting bookmarks at Genesis 1, Job 1, and Matthew 1 and reading one chapter of each every day. This way you read the Old Testament through once and the New Testament through twice during the year. This was the first plan I tried, but there are many other plans just as helpful. Nevertheless, reading the entire Bible brings God's Word alive. Systematically reading all of it embeds God's Word firmly in our hearts, minds, souls, and lives.

Often we are tempted to avoid the Old Testament. I was reminded just recently in reading Philip Yancey's *The*

Bible Jesus Read just how valuable the Old Testament is. It teaches so much about God the Father, even as the New Testament shows Him as God the Son and God the Holy Spirit. The Old Testament writers so vividly show us that God is a God Who acts in history. The Old Testament unfolds God's plan of forgiveness and redemption, which culminates in the New Testament. It shows God as very personal, a God Who enters our lives and loves us. It teaches that life with God is individual, personal, and intimate.

By reading the Bible, all of it, we find guidance for living the forgiven life.

Forgetting the Past and Moving on with Life

Basketball star David Robinson clearly demonstrates God's life-transforming power as he works with deprived children and plays on the National Basketball Association's San Antonio Spurs team. Though Robinson was taken to church regularly as a child, he drifted away from his roots. Instead he found success and satisfaction in many others ways—giftedness in playing the piano, computer and electronics skills, a good life and achievement at the US Naval Academy, and a career in professional basketball. After fulfilling his obligation to the navy for his education, Robinson was drafted by the Spurs. Fame and fortune grabbed his attention. He became a superstar center in the NBA, though a championship alluded Robinson and his team.

As happens to many of us, the Holy Spirit continued to work in Robinson's life. Basketball, cars, houses, women—none of these gave him any sense of direction in life. A minister provided spiritual guidance to Robinson, and in 1991, he became a follower of Christ. His new faith led him back to a former girlfriend who was a vibrant Christian, and with her he established a Christian home. Robinson claimed that everything in his life, even basketball, had new meaning and purpose after he found Christ as his Savior.

Robinson became a role model for children, a good example they could follow. He poured himself into the lives of poor and deprived children in a predominantly African American and Hispanic section of San Antonio. Not only did he seek and find ways to use his abundant resources to provide better education and better lives, but also he invested himself in the community and spent time with the children personally.

When the Spurs selected a top pick in the NBA draft, Robinson showed the magnanimity of a Christ follower. Rather than sulking or trying to torpedo his rival, Robinson mentored the young man. They worked together for the good of the team rather than pitting themselves against each other. Robinson did everything he could to help the new star succeed, as well as helping the Spurs finally win an NBA championship. He exhibited many of the characteristics of a kingdom person spelled out in God's Word.[2]

If we are to be obedient and productive in God's work, we must forget the past and move on with life, as did David Robinson. Only then can we take the direction God wants. The present and future need our focus, not the past. A friend recently remarked to me that when we thank God for the gift of a new day, we are actually thanking Him for the present.

Do you ever have trouble letting go of the past and moving on with life today? Paul gave good advice about moving on in doing God's work in his letter to the Philippians:

"I have not yet reached my goal, and I am not perfect. . . . So I keep on running and struggling to take hold of the prize. My friends, I don't feel that I have already arrived.

<u>But I forget what is behind, and I struggle for what is ahead</u>. *I run toward the goal, so that I can win the prize of being called to heaven"* (Phil. 3:12–14, author's emphasis).

Paul's final goal was to be with God in heaven. But he determined to keep on fully running the race for God while still on earth.

What about your daily life and its challenges and opportunities? God's Word gives us help and sound advice in this area, too. Isaiah gave the Israelites a word from God about running the daily race when they were held captive in Babylonia. The Israelites would soon be allowed to return home. Isaiah reassured them that God is all-powerful and in complete control. He gives strength for daily life, never gets tired or weary, and has wisdom that cannot be measured (Isa. 40:21–28). Isaiah offers this word about moving on:

"The Lord gives strength to those who are weary. Even young people get tired, then stumble and fall. But those who trust the Lord will find new strength. They will be strong like eagles soaring upward on wings, they will walk and run without getting tired" (Isa. 40:29–31).

Does anything ever bog you down? Are you still challenged by sin? The writer of Hebrews admonished Christ followers to get rid of anything that slows them down, especially sin. "We must be determined to run the race that is ahead of us. We must keep our eyes on Jesus, who leads us and makes our faith complete" (Heb. 12:1–2).

God gives us His strength so that we can be strong in following Him and living the forgiven life. Paul describes the armor or battle gear God gives us to put on so we can be prepared and equipped to stand up against Satan's attacks and trickery. Satan has evil spiritual forces and we need God's protection to both defend ourselves and to go on the offensive. Though we do not physically wear armor like the New Testament soldier did, we need the equipment Paul describes as we are engaged in spiritual warfare. God's equipment for battle against Satan, which He wears and supplies to us, includes:

- A belt of truth and a breastplate of righteousness: faithful devotion to Christ's cause, loyalty to God, and always doing what is right.
- Shoes: firm and sure footing of the desire or readiness to tell the good news about peace.
- A shield of faith that will stop Satan's flaming arrows: complete confidence in and trust of God.
- A helmet of God's saving power.
- A sword of the Holy Spirit, which is God's message to be proclaimed.
- Constant prayer as the Holy Spirit prompts, asking for God's help for whatever you are doing, to never give up, and for all of God's people (Eph. 6:10–18).

A Job to Do

Scriptures repeatedly remind us that God has given us a job to do. As Jesus was about to leave earth and ascend to the Father after His death and resurrection, He gave specific instructions to His followers for all time, telling us what we must do. Often called the Great Commission, Matthew records it this way in his Gospel:

"I have been given all authority in heaven and on earth! Go to the people of all nations and make them my disciples. Baptize them in the name of the Father, the Son, and the Holy Spirit, and teach them to do everything I have told you. I will be with you always, even until the end of the world" (Matt. 28:18–20).

Mark (16:14–18), Luke (24:36–49; Acts 1:6–8), and John (20:19–23) each repeat these important instructions from Jesus.

Jesus still gives the command to follow Him today. His commission to His followers is still to take the good news to all nations or peoples of the world, beginning where we live (called Jerusalem in the Scriptures), then spreading out into the entire world (Judea, Samaria, and "the uttermost parts of the world"). Some Christ followers call this missions. Others call it evangelism. No matter what we call our job, it involves taking the message of His good news to everyone in the entire world.

Paul states the job we are to do in another way. As Christ followers, we are to be involved in the task or business of reconciliation. We are to take the message of God's peace and forgiveness to others:

"Anyone who belongs to Christ is a new person. The past is forgotten, and everything is new. God has done it all! He sent Christ to make peace between himself and us, and he has given us the work of making peace between himself and others. What we mean is that God was in Christ, offering peace and forgiveness to the people of this world. And he has given us the work of sharing his message about peace" (2 Cor. 5:17–19).

Forgiveness frees each of us to do what God has called us to do. The Bible illustrates this freedom vividly in the lives of the many persons who received God's forgiveness. Jesus cast demons out of two men from the town of Gadara. The people nearby immediately ran into town to tell everyone what Jesus had done (Matt. 8:28–34). He brought redemption and reconciliation to the Samaritan woman at the well. She ran into town to tell this story. He forgave David, Peter, and Paul, and they became tremendous leaders in the story of God's redeeming work. He forgave His chosen people time and time again so they could fulfill His mission for Him.

God has forgiven us, the Christ followers of today, for a reason. He has work for each of us to do: the work of ministry and witness, the work of missions, the work of reconciliation. We can each be useful in His kingdom. He gives us the strength and stamina to stick with the task, even in times of great stress, turmoil, transition, and difficulty.

What does God want you to do? What is your task? Your mission is between you and God. Nevertheless, it is a divine calling. I particularly like Paul's prayer from his letter to the Ephesians where he expresses in beautiful terms Christ's love for us. When I am down or discouraged, this prayer reminds me that I can live a forgiven life.

"I kneel in prayer to the Father. All beings in heaven and on earth receive their life from him. God is wonderful and glorious. I pray that his Spirit will make you become strong followers and that Christ will live in your hearts because of your faith. Stand firm and be deeply rooted in his love. I pray that you and all of God's people will understand what is called wide or long or high or deep. I want you to know all about Christ's love, although it is too wonderful to be measured. Then your lives will be filled with all that God is.

"I pray that Christ Jesus and the church will forever bring praise to God. His power at work in us can do far more than we dare ask or imagine. Amen" (Eph. 3:14–21).

The forgiven life involves faith, love, and strength. Then our lives will be filled with all that God is and enabled to do what He wants us to do.

As I came to the end of my reflections on God's forgiveness as an act of His grace and mercy, I wanted to join other Christians in pouring out my soul to Him in worship. I could almost visualize a great choir, wearing beautiful robes and singing a majestic anthem. In this choir were not only the heavenly hosts and all those in Christendom who had already gone to be with the Lord, but God's current saints on earth today—you and me. In voices of beautiful harmony and accompanied by a full orchestra, these are the words we sang:

Marvelous grace of our Loving Lord,
Grace that exceeds our sin and our guilt,
Yonder on Calvary's mount outpoured,
There where the blood of the Lamb was spilt.

Dark is the stain that we cannot hide,
What can avail to wash it away?
Look! There is flowing a crimson tide;
Whiter than snow you may be today.

Marvelous, infinite, matchless grace,
Freely bestowed on all who believe;
All who are longing to see His face,
Will you this moment His grace receive?

Grace, grace, God's grace,
Grace that will pardon and cleanse within;
Grace, grace, God's grace,
Grace that is greater than all our sin.[3]

Questions for Thought and Discussion

1. Read the Sermon on the Mount (Matt. 5–7) in a modern translation such as *The Message, Contemporary English Version, New Living Translation,* or another one of your choice. What is the most important thing you learned while reading the Sermon on the Mount? What are one or two areas of your life that you want to improve? What are some practical steps you can take immediately to do so?

2. How is Paul's advice in Romans 13:8 to 15:6 helpful for twenty-first-century Christ followers today? What piece of advice is especially helpful to you? Why?

3. What do Paul's writings teach about relationships? What do you think are the most important character traits you need in your relationships with your spouse, other family members, friends, boss or co-workers, fellow church members, and unbelievers? Why?

4. What helps you avoid temptation? How do you apply this help?

5. What is your plan for ongoing and systematic study and reading of the Bible? If you don't already have a plan, how will you start one?

6. What is your goal for running life's race?

7. What enables you to live life each day by moving on?

8. After His resurrection, what did Jesus tell His followers to do? What does this message mean to Jesus' followers today? What did Paul mean when he told us to take God's peace and forgiveness to others? What does this mean to you?

9. What has God called you to do in His kingdom? How are you following through on this call?

---

[1] *Life Application Study Bible*, New International Version (Wheaton, IL: Tyndale House Publishers, Inc., 1991), 1651–61; *The Learning Bible*, Contemporary English Version (New York: American Bible Society, 2000), 1744–52; Clair M. Crissey, *Layman's Bible Book Commentary* (Nashville: Broadman Press, 1981), 15:30–49.
[2] Lynn Rosellini, "Passing It Back," *Reader's Digest*, April 2001, 94–101.
[3] "Grace Greater than Our Sin" (*Baptist Hymnal*).

About the writer
Bobbie Sorrill Patterson, a native of Washington, D.C., is a magna cum laude graduate of Carson-Newman College and holds a master of arts in religious education degree from Southwestern Baptist Theological Seminary and a master of arts degree from the University of Maryland. She is the author of *WMU—A Church Missions Organization* and *Annie Armstrong: Dreamer in Action*. She also wrote the *Ruth and Naomi Project Guide* for WMU of Virginia.

Bobbie retired in August 2000 as associate executive director of Woman's Missionary Union, Auxiliary to Southern Baptist Convention. In her last assignment she was deployed to Richmond, Virginia, to work with the WMU of Virginia to implement a missions network plan to offer a place for women in all Baptist churches in Virginia, and to coordinate WMU's involvement in Impact Northeast. In retirement she serves as volunteer coordinator of the Ruth and Naomi Project, a WMU of Virginia ministry to develop missions leaders.

Married to the late Arthur Patterson, Bobbie has three stepdaughters and two granddaughters.